The Social Psychology
of Tourist Behaviour

INTERNATIONAL SERIES IN EXPERIMENTAL SOCIAL PSYCHOLOGY

Series Editor: Michael Argyle, University of Oxford

Vol 1.   BOCHNER
         Cultures in Contact

Vol 2.   HOWITT
         The Mass Media and Social Problems

Vol 3.   PEARCE
         The Social Psychology of Tourist Behaviour

A Related Pergamon Journal
LANGUAGE & COMMUNICATION*
An Interdisciplinary Journal

Editor: Roy Harris, *University of Oxford*

The primary aim of the journal is to fill the need for a publicational forum devoted to the discussion of topics and issues in communication which are of interdisciplinary significance. It will publish contributions from researchers in all fields relevant to the study of verbal and non-verbal communication.

Emphasis will be placed on the implications of current research for establishing common theoretical frameworks within which findings from different areas of study may be accommodated and interrelated.

By focusing attention on the many ways in which language is integrated with other forms of communicational activity and interactional behaviour it is intended to explore ways of developing a science of communication which is not restricted by existing disciplinary boundaries.

* Free specimen copy available on request.

NOTICE TO READERS

Dear Reader

An Invitation to Publish in and Recommend the Placing of a Standing Order to Volumes Published in this Valuable Series.

If your library is not already a standing/continuation order customer to this series, may we recommend that you place a standing/continuation order to receive immediately upon publication all new volumes. Should you find that these volumes no longer serve your needs, your order can be cancelled at any time without notice.

The Editors and the Publisher will be glad to receive suggestions or outlines of suitable titles, reviews or symposia for editorial consideration: if found acceptable, rapid publication is guaranteed.

ROBERT MAXWELL
Publisher at Pergamon Press

The Social Psychology of Tourist Behaviour

BY

PHILIP L. PEARCE

PERGAMON PRESS

OXFORD · NEW YORK · TORONTO · SYDNEY · PARIS · FRANKFURT

U.K.	Pergamon Press Ltd., Headington Hill Hall, Oxford OX3 0BW, England
U.S.A	Pergamon Press Inc., Maxwell House, Fairview Park, Elmsford, New York 10523, U.S.A.
CANADA	Pergamon Press Canada Ltd., Suite 104, 150 Consumers Road, Willowdale, Ontario M2J 1P9, Canada
AUSTRALIA	Pergamon Press (Aust.) Pty. Ltd., P.O. Box 544, Potts Point, N.S.W. 2011, Australia
FRANCE	Pergamon Press SARL, 24 rue des Ecoles, 75240 Paris, Cedex 05, France
FEDERAL REPUBLIC OF GERMANY	Pergamon Press GmbH, 6242 Kronberg-Taunus, Hammerweg 6, Federal Republic of Germany

First edition 1982

Library of Congress Cataloging in Publication Data
Pearce, Philip L.
The social psychology of tourist behavior.
(International series in experimental social psychology; v. 3)
Includes bibliographical references.
1. Travelers—Psychology. 2. Tourist trade—
Psychological aspects. I. Title. II. Series.
G156.P4   1982   910.4'01'9   81–23456

British Library Cataloguing in Publication Data
Pearce, Philip L.
The social psychology of tourist behaviour.—
(International series in experimental social psychology; 3)
1. Tourist trade   2. Social psychology
I. Title   II. Series
302   BF57
ISBN 0–08–025794–1

Printed in Great Britain by A. Wheaton & Co. Ltd.

Introduction to the Series

MICHAEL ARGYLE

Social psychology is in a very interesting period, and one of rapid development. It has survived a number of "crises", there is increased concern with external validity and relevance to the real world, the repertoire of research methods and statistical procedures has been greatly extended, and a number of exciting new ideas and approaches are being tried out.

The books in this series present some of these new developments; each volume contains a balance of new material and a critical review of the relevant literature. The new material consists of empirical research, research procedures, theoretical formulations, or a combination of these. Authors have been asked to review and evaluate the often very extensive past literature, and to explain their new findings, methods or theories clearly.

The authors are from all over the world, and have been very carefully chosen, mainly on the basis of their previous published work, showing the importance and originality of their contribution, and their ability to present it clearly. Some of these books report a programme of research by one individual or a team, some are based on doctoral theses, others on conferences.

Social psychologists have moved into an increasing number of applied fields, and a growing number of practitioners have made use of our work. All the books in this series will have some practical application, some will be on topics of wide popular interest, as well as adding to scientific knowledge. The books in the series are designed for advanced undergraduates, graduate students and relevant practitioners, and in some cases for a rather broader public.

We do not know how social psychology will develop, and it takes quite a variety of forms already. However it is a great pleasure to be associated with books by some of those social psychologists who are developing the subject in such interesting ways.

Acknowledgements

I would like to acknowledge the contributions of the following people to this volume. Nerina Caltabiano was extremely helpful in her role as research assistant. Barbara de Rome provided valuable library assistance, while Dr Mike Smithson's statistical creativity deserves special mention. Professor George Kearney, Head of the Behavioural Sciences Department at James Cook University, supported this research wherever possible. Dr Michael Argyle and the staff of Pergamon Press have been encouraging throughout. Personal acknowledgements are gratefully recorded: to my parents for stimulating an interest in travel, to Sharyn for her understanding and to Susan for her infectious enthusiasm. Finally, the contributions of the numerous tourists who provided the attitudes and experiences which have been explored here are sincerely acknowledged.

Contents

1

Tourists, Tourism and Tourist Psychology

Introduction

The literature and research on tourism is a fascinating mixture, covering a vast range of ideas and issues. Not surprisingly, a large number of the studies are concerned with economic issues and debates, but there are also some contributions from geographers, anthropologists, sociologists and occasionally psychologists. Interesting information concerning tourism is also contained in travel guides, tourist brochures, tourist authority publications and the anecdotal accounts of travellers. The person who familiarizes himself with this literature is immediately struck by a curious paradox. Tourism is a huge multinational enterprise which is of central importance to the economies of many countries and yet it has generated relatively few detailed academic studies, particularly in the behavioural sciences.

It appears that many types of field researchers—and this includes anthropologists, sociologists and psychologists—have simply tried to ignore the impacts and presence of tourism and tourists. For these researchers tourists are simply a nuisance, an annoying reminder that most primitive or interesting societies are now highly accessible to the modern world. Like weeds in the garden plot, tourists spoil the character of the researcher's carefully cultivated community. Further, the literature which is produced by the tourists is seen as limited and uninteresting. Claude Levi-Strauss (1976) comments:

> What do we find in the travel books? We are told the exact number of packing cases that was required, or about the misdemeanours of the ship's dog, and interspersed among the anecdotes are scraps of hackneyed information which have appeared in every textbook in the past fifty years and are presented with remarkable effrontery as valid evidence or even original discoveries. No doubt there are exceptions and every period has had its genuine travellers. (p. 16)

The paradox concerning modern tourism, and until very recently a failure to study it seriously, may well relate to deeply embedded values in Western

1

society about play and work. Protestant cultural prescriptions have emphasized the value of hard work as a spiritual, or at least noble, cause for humanity. This emphasis has effectively devalued play and leisure as cultural pursuits which in turn may be responsible for the lack of research interest. Indeed, as Huizinga claimed as long ago as 1938:

> For the adult and responsible human being play is a function which he could equally well leave alone. Play is superfluous. The need for it is only urgent to the extent that the enjoyment of it makes it a need. Play can be deferred or suspended at any time. It is never imposed by physical necessity or moral duty. It is never a task. (p. 26)

It is a small step from the view that play is a superfluous activity in responsible society to one which considers the study of play and leisure to be a peripheral research field. It could only be the frivolous who would want to study play, only frustrated travellers and those seeking cheap holidays who would wish to explore tourism.

In addition, other negative views of tourist research have probably contributed to the slow development of behavioural science interest. For example, since tourism is inextricably linked with capitalism the would-be researcher also attracts the attacks of concerned left-wing forces. Here the criticism may focus on the researchers' role in aiding the exploitation of people and the degradation of the environment. It is not surprising then that these societal values and criticisms have tended to deflect the aspirations of scholars inclined to study tourism. Of course the dearth of research is also attributable to other causes. Until recently there have not been recognized academic positions in this field, the need for tourist research was not recognized, as tourism seemed to be a trouble-free, clean industry, and there were few established paradigms concerning how to tackle such a vast phenomenon. For all that, it remains astonishing that one of the world's biggest industries gives rise to only a handful of books and journal articles each year.

It is necessary to sample briefly the existing literature on tourism in order to understand the role of the present volume. This chapter will be concerned with economic, geographical, anthropological and other approaches to tourism. It will attempt to give a rounded image of each of these methods of inquiry as they pertain to tourism, but will necessarily be a brief overview of these approaches. Several of the themes discussed will be dealt with in greater detail in later chapters since many aspects of social psychological enquiry are closely related to concerns in these other disciplines.

Economic studies of tourism

Tourism may be defined as the loosely interrelated amalgam of industries which arise from the movement of people, and their stay in various destinations outside of their home area. Burkart and Medlik (1974) point out that the movements which characterize tourism are of a short-term nature and that the traveller is not concerned with seeking employment. Tourism is, in essence, a phenomenon concerned with the leisured society at play.

A neat and precise definition of the tourist, as opposed to tourism, has continually proved to be a problem for researchers concerned with tourism economics and statistics. A United Nations conference on travel and tourism held in Rome in 1963 proposed that tourists were temporary visitors staying at least 24 hours in the country visited. The purpose of their journey must be able to be classified under one of the following headings: leisure (including recreation, holiday, health, study, religion and sport) or business, family visits and conferences. From this definition it appears that nearly every traveller is a tourist. The Rome conference also added a category called excursionist which comprised temporary visitors staying less than 24 hours in the country visited (including travellers on cruises). These definitions are clearly geared for appraising passport statistics, measuring large flows of tourist traffic and distinguishing tourists from migrants and seasonal workers. It is also apparent that a great variety of travellers are being falsely labelled as "tourists" in the above definitions. It will be argued later that these passport-type definitions are too broad to be of use in mapping out a psychological understanding of tourist behaviour. Several of the above-categories of people (e.g. businessmen, sportsmen, conference travellers) are not perceived, either by themselves or by others, as tourists. A critical aspect of the tourist role is the phenomenological realization that one is acting as, and being perceived as, a transient figure with no enduring relationship to the visited community. For the present it is useful to explore the kinds of studies conducted with these internationally recognized passport-type definitions of the tourist.

Tourism and the tourist are, at least from a research perspective, separate entities. One can study the economic well-being of a number of travel-related industries without ever really concerning oneself with the individual tourist. Similarly, the tourist's financial capabilities, that is his or her capacity to purchase holidays, can be investigated without exploring the precise contexts in which the holidays take place. An interesting illustration of the first approach is the concern with what has been termed the tourist multiplier index. This concept refers to the amount of money generated in a community from each unit of currency the tourist spends in that community. For example, Archer and Owen (1972), using a complex weighted formula to balance tourist income from services purchased against community expenditure to provide those services, produced a set of tourist regional multipliers for the Welsh county of Anglesey. For hotel and guest visitors the multiplier was calculated to be 1·25 which can be interpreted as suggesting that for every £1 of tourist spending 25 pence worth of income is generated after the costs to the community have been extracted. It is noticeable that those tourists who use more local services and goods, rather than national or extra-regional products, generate more returns for the visited area. Thus, the multipliers for bed and breakfast and farmhouse visitors was calculated as 1·58 while for camping visitors it was 1·35.

The calculation of economic indices such as the regional tourist multiplier is simplest when the region being studied can be clearly defined and where the flows of income in an out of the region are relatively easy to trace. Smith and Wilde (1977) calculated a set of regional multipliers for Western Tasmania and reported multiplier levels for this small regional economy similar to those found by Archer and Owen in Wales. This economic information can be seen as an important aid in the formulation of government policies on tourism. It directs attention to the place of tourism in the regional economy and the kind of tourism which is most beneficial economically, and can help to justify government expenditure on tourist-related facilities.

National as well as regional tourist multipliers may be calculated. These figures are undoubtedly less precise than those calculated for small communities where the cash flows are more easily observed. But the estimates do make interesting reading. For the Pacific the figure is reputed to be 3·2, for Ireland 2·7, for Greece 1·2–1·4 and for Hawaii 0·9–1·3 (Burkart and Medlik, 1974). While methodological problems may account for some of the variation in these figures, it would appear that the economic benefits of tourism can vary considerably. For those Pacific islands where tourists content themselves with cheaply produced local goods and pay high prices for these services, tourism can significantly boost the local economy. When tourists require expensive imported foods and clothes, and demand sophisticated accommodation, the impact on the economy is markedly diminished. The figure of 0·9 for Hawaii indicates that in some circumstances the tourist demands so much that the regional economy may actually be paying to keep tourists in their community. That is, the cost of providing airport facilities, hotels, roads, sewerage, combating pollution, paying wages and purchasing consumer goods may exceed the income generated by the tourist presence. And of course this deficit refers to the economic side of tourism, not the social costs which do not enter into the multiplier calculations.

Inherent in these economic studies of tourism multipliers is a very limited concept of the tourist. The concern of the researchers is with total tourist expenditure and thus they are indifferent to the kinds of tourists in the area, their age, sex, motivation for travelling and the quality of the goods and services they receive.

Apart from attempting to assess the overall benefit of tourism to a community, economic research has also been directed towards such topics as tourist demand, marketing, forecasting, planning and development. The bulk of the published literature on tourism falls under one or more of these economic areas of interest. Again the emphasis here is on tourism rather than the tourist and his experiences, though research in these areas gets a little closer to the individual by seeking attitudes to hotels, airlines, and destination areas. Studies of tourist demand, for example, cover a huge range of topics and may embrace everything from where tourists like hotels to be located to their preferences for soap and toilet paper (Blomstrom, 1967; Arbel and Pizam, 1977).

On a larger scale demand and development studies are concerned with why some countries and areas are more appealing to the tourist than others. These kinds of enquiries are closely linked to the work of some geographers who have also investigated the nature of regional images and the aesthetics of landscape evaluation (cf. Dunn, 1974). The flavour and scope of these studies may be illustrated by one or two representative cases.

Gearing, Swart and Var (1974) point out that government investment in the tourist industry should be directed towards those areas which have the power to attract the greatest number of visitors. Such assessments of regional tourist attractiveness can be quantified and the authors report a case study empirically assessing 65 geographical units in Turkey. The techniques of the study are of some interest because they illustrate the kinds of assumptions made about tourists and tourist behaviour by those working within an economic resource assessment framework. The authors assume there are 17 criteria relevant to tourist attractiveness. These cohere into five larger units: natural factors, social indices, historical components, recreational and shopping facilities, and the infrastructure for tourist comfort. This selection, which represents the views of the researchers rather than the tourists, omits such factors as the presence of other tourists and language difficulties. But such omissions are not as serious as the next assumption. The writers used 26 tourism experts who ranked the 17 criteria in the way that the tourists would. While such a sampling substitution is obviously cheap and expedient, the error introduced by assuming that a certain group of people know how tourists behave and feel could well be totally distorting the results of the study. Having established a ranking of the 17 criteria, other governmental officials rated the areas on these criteria, thus enabling a total tourist attractiveness index for each region of the counting to be established. Such an approach then enables explicit quantified comparisons among tourist regions.

Other work concerned with resource evaluation and the assessment of tourist demand shows a little more sophistication. For example Ferrario (1979a, 1979b) has mapped out tourist regions of South Africa using a comprehensive and highly praised methodology. This work, which won a travel research award, establishes an index of tourist potential by considering the interplay of tourist demand, expressed by visitors' preferences, and tourist supply which is evaluated on the basis of the ability of the resource to be used for tourism. International travellers leaving South Africa were sampled over a 12-month period in order to determine their preference patterns for 21 tourist attractions (e.g. scenery and landscape, wildlife, etc.). Then 2300 tourist sites were given evaluation ratings by multiplying the tourists' preferences for the 21 attractions with the extent to which the sites provided those attractions. Guidebooks were used to provide one half of Ferrario's assessment system—the evaluation of the resource in terms of demand. He then uses six criteria: seasonality, accessibility, admission, importance, fragility, and popularity, in his assessment of the capacity of the resource to supply the demands of the tourists. A total supply score for each site was calculated by weighting the relative importance of these criteria with the extent to which the site is characterized by the criteria. Next, an index combining the demand and supply scores is calculated. Tourist regions with a high demand score and a high supply score receive high tourist potential scores. The efficiency of Ferrario's method is said to be supported by a correlation between his tourist potential index and the current network of tour operations in South Africa.

The reasons for this kind of work being popular are clear. Provided one has access to reasonably large funds a set of easy-to-read indices can be obtained on a regional, national or even international scale. Since these indices will tend to correlate with current levels of tourist activity in a region the researcher feels reassured that his methodology is sound. In addition it may be giving him something to say by highlighting one or two as yet underdeveloped regions. A critical appraisal of this work would suggest that while it has much potential, at least one major caveat should be noted. The tourist potential index is a hybrid animal containing in its pedigree equally weighted demand and supply scores. Thus regions with high demand and low supply, or low demand and high supply will, unless one bothers to examine the figures, be indistinguishable in the final analysis. They would hardly seem to be equivalent in the everyday meaning of the term tourist potential. As a further comment it is interesting to note the writer's sense of tourist psychology. He comments in calculating the supply side of his index that the popularity of a site is an asset over less populated sites because tourists "follow the herd instinct". It seems that even amongst tourism researchers the tourist is not held in very high esteem if this Springbok type metaphor is taken seriously.

While some economic studies of demand and supply may be criticized for their generality many others are narrowly focused and fully aware of their particular limitations. For example Goodrich (1977) has analysed the demands and preferences for tourist destinations held by American Express travellers. He found that these were concerned, in order, with entertainment, purchasing opportunities and then climate in their holiday preferences. The middle-class, white and income biases of the sample are carefully noted. This kind of marketing segmentation study of tourists' preferences and desires has many advocates (Mayo, 1975; Hawes, 1977; Solomon and George, 1977; Schewe and Calatone, 1978). Marketing segmentation is a basic component of national approaches to tourist demand and advertising. The British Tourist Authority has conducted numerous studies of visitors to Britain according to nationality, age and social class divisions (British Tourist Authority *Research Newsletters*, 1972–80). Similarly, the Canadian Government Office of Tourism has studied the profiles of visitors to Canada while the U.S. Department of Commerce has data on the travel behaviours of most European national groups who visit North America. Understanding the travel scene by examining the activities of particular market groups is a theme which is also frequently explored in travel research conferences (The Travel Research Association, 1972–80). More detailed discussion of this work will be undertaken in a later discussion of tourist motivation and attitudes, where it will be seen to be a useful starting point for developing psychological studies of tourist behaviour.

Other concerns of the economic writing on tourism have been with the impact of political and economic changes such as the energy crisis on reshaping tourist demand (Solomon and George, 1976; Corsi and Harvey, 1979). This complicated and constantly evolving issue may have far-reaching consequences in reshaping the nature of tourist demand.

Economic studies on tourism can be viewed from many perspectives other than those already discussed. For example, there are national economic studies of tourism for almost every major tourist country. A good example of this kind of work is Bryden's study of the Caribbean where he attempts to assess fully the costs and advantages of tourism to the West Indian community (Bryden, 1973). Unlike many other students of tourist activity, Bryden emphasizes the need to study the human aspect of tourism, for he sees this as a necessary cost when the local population is relatively poor and unsophisticated. As well as country-by-country analyses there are detailed studies of the component industries—hotels, airlines, shipping, trains, car hire, restaurants—which depend heavily on tourist traffic. A broad perspective of these contacts is presented by Waters' yearly summary entitled *The Big Picture* which offers a concise statistical account of travel trends (Waters, 1980). This volume provides a kind of yearly *Guinness Book of Records* account of tourist activity and the reader may glean such facts as each airline's percentage of the U.S.–Europe air market, the numbers of tourists visiting each major tourist country, the rates of growth of tourism in a myriad of locations and the profitability of the world's major hotel chains.

How are these economic studies inadequate from the perspective of a psychology of tourist behaviour? As suggested already, they rarely conceive of the tourist as anything more than a money-dispensing machine which requires regular servicing. The feelings, memories, frustrations, aspirations and disappointments of the tourist are therefore lost in this mechanistic analysis of supply and demand. Interactions with the local people are seen as monetary exchanges rather than the sometimes painful, sometimes beneficial contacts between cultures. Even where the individual tourist is approached and his attitudes sought, the topics researched are only the tourists' consumer preferences. The end result is often what 1000 tourists think about 100 topics that the market researcher thought tourists should think about. The tourist's own perspective on the situation is all too frequently lost. At times, as in the evaluation of tourist demand through resource appraisal, the opinions of those who know tourists are substituted for the views of the tourists themselves. Nearly all the economic studies are conducted in isolation in that there is little building on previous research and analysis. This failure to provide a cumulative body of research reflects the heavy market survey orientation of the economic studies. The myth of the tourist mob also persists in some accounts. This view sees tourists as of a lesser species, liable to follow herd instincts and likely to conform to the latest fashions in travel destinations. One feels after reading economic accounts of tourism that travelling is a matter of passport statistics, demand and supply, and economic returns. Clearly these are central to tourism but so is the experience of the tourist. The economic studies of tourism highlight the need but provide only a few of the stepping stones towards formulating a psychological understanding of the tourist.

Geographical studies of tourism

Perhaps more than any other group of researchers, geographers have highlighted the regional and spatial imbalances which accompany tourism. One of the issues of interest has been why similar regions and countries have markedly different tourism statistics. For instance why does Spain receive almost twelve times more visitors than Greece (Robinson, 1976, p. 245) and why does Austria attract five times more visitors than the Soviet Union (Waters, 1980)? While spatial and locational factors account for some of these differences there is a general recognition that publicity, and the creation of a favourable image, shape the tourist flows of the World (Williams and Zelinsky, 1970; Cosgrove and Jackson, 1972). Accordingly, research attempts have been directed at investigating the comparative images of tourist destination areas. This kind of destination and resource appraisal work has already been illustrated in part by the work of Gearing, Swart and Var (1974) in Turkey and Ferrario (1979a, 1979b) in South Africa.

Several methodologies have been employed to document the images of tourist destination areas. These include the computation of a comparative index (Gearing, Swart and Var, 1974; Ferrario, 1979a, 1979b), the presentation of profiles along semantic differential scales (Hunt, 1975), the use of spatial mapping as in multidimensional scaling (Anderssen and Colberg,

1973) and repertory grid analysis (Riley and Palmer, 1976). The kinds of images produced by these analyses are illustrated in Figure 1.1.

Such images of tourist destinations depend a good deal on the sample of tourists chosen. Age and class differences appear to be major determinants of the composition of these regional images (cf. BTA *Holiday Motivations Study*, 1974). The variable of social class is of particular interest in characterizing tourist locations.

It is possible when examining the role of tourism in any one location to observe a sequence of tourist phases. Christaller (1964) observed that many kinds of tourism favour peripheral locations, places which are removed from the urban and industrial concentrations. This is particularly valid for tourism based on natural resources (the seas, mountains, remote landscapes) and where the motivation to travel is partly to escape urban life. To travel to peripheral, distant locations requires money and time. Thus, many tourist locations begin their existence as the haunts of the aristocracy who have followed the earlier footsteps of adventurers, explorers and scientists. The aristocratic phase of a tourist resort may be short-lived if the price of reaching this destination soon falls within the economic compass of the middle class. For example Nash (1979), observing the rise and fall of Nice as an aristocratic tourist culture, observes that "with the arrival of increasing numbers of lower ranking bourgeois and people of doubtful reputation [Nice] began to lose some of its aristocratic cachet" (p. 67). A similar story of decline could be applied to such diverse centres as Acapulco, Blackpool, and Majorca. In turn, the middle-class invasion may be displaced. Package deals and greater disposal of wealth may enable working-class groups to aspire to and succeed in visiting the once aristocratic haunts. Thus the arrival of the workers displaces the middle class. Places such as Majorca, Scarborough, Brighton, Blackpool, the Costa Brava, Torremolinos, to name just a few examples, develop a working-class focus, crowding large numbers of people into the hotel rooms once selectively allocated to the wealthy. This process, which may be termed successive class intrusion, can be seen operating at both the regional and international level. In locations which are extremely attractive to tourists, such as cities like Paris and London, the geographical retreat of the aristocracy and the middle class is less spectacular. Instead such tourists buy their social distinctiveness by locating themselves in the more expensive hotels located in the most favourable positions of the city.

It is likely that the process of successive class intrusion in the original sense of tourists relocating themselves is on the decline. The costs of international air fares now provide less of a class barrier shaping holiday travel patterns and many different types of tourist can reach the same location. If the above pattern of analysis is correct it would suggest that the social demarcations within these accessible tourist areas will probably increase by encouraging zones of price-controlled exclusivity.

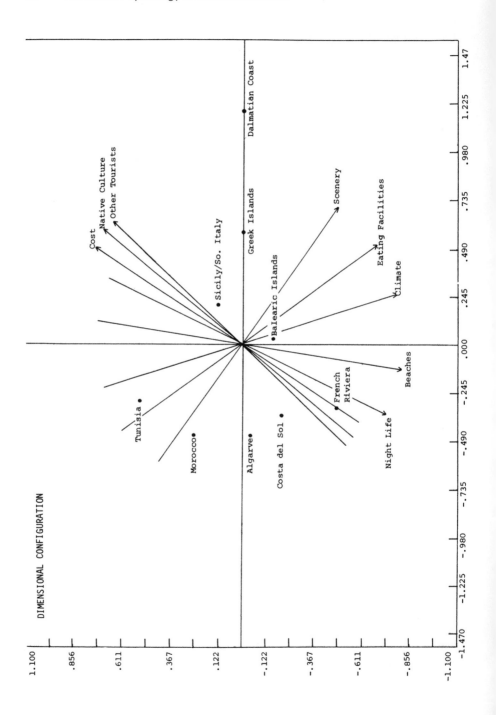

DIMENSIONAL CONFIGURATION

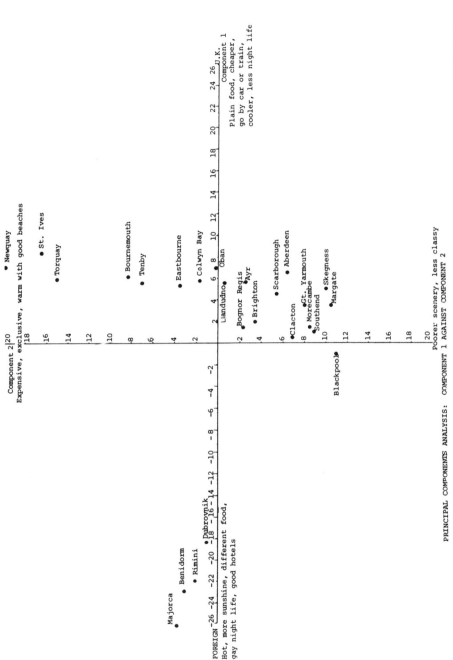

FIG. 1.1   Two approaches to image analysis. **A**: The use of multidimensional scaling to provide images of Mediterranean resorts (after Anderssen and Colberg, 1973). **B**: The use of repertory grid analysis to provide images of seaside resorts (after Riley and Palmer, 1976).

This geographical study of tourist regions prompts interesting questions about the travel motivations of different groups of tourists. How important are status and social class considerations in the motivational structure of different groups of tourists? Is the frequent phenomenon of tourists reporting that they dislike other tourists related to the social class intrusion patterns discussed above? Clearly these geographical studies on tourism have prompted questions which an adequate social psychological account of tourist behaviour must attempt to explain. Efforts directed towards this goal will take place in a chapter discussing tourist motivation.

As well as concerning themselves with the spatial analysis of tourism, geographers see tourism's influence on landscape morphology and town design as a part of their interest area. For example, D. Pearce (1978) studied French resort towns and concluded that the form of these tourism-dominated areas had a particular functional logic. He noted the interpenetration of dwellings, the sea and boat moorings in such resorts. This kind of development, which is termed a "cité lacustre", is the result of a planned effort to integrate the most important aspects of the environment for the resort owner. Such new designs tend to privatize the sea-shore, hindering public participation and leading to spatial segregation amongst different classes of holiday-maker. Several geographers have also shown that beach resorts tend to foster lateral, strip-like development (Gilbert, 1939; 1949; Smailes, 1953; Robinson, 1976). A striking example of such a development is the Surfers Paradise strip in Southern Queensland, Australia (see Figure 1.2).

Geographers have also been concerned with the country-side and the physical features of the landscape which attract tourists. Frequently they have been interested in resource appraisal, as in the economic geographical studies reviewed earlier, but they have also been concerned with environmental damage and degradation caused by tourists and tourist developments (Cohen, 1978). However, the study of the physical environment as a determinant and influence on behaviour is also a fundamental concern of psychologists. The geographer's interests in environmental perception, orientation in the environment and tourists' reactions to scenery are also fundamental concerns of the environmental psychologist. Since the latter discipline may be conceived as a form of applied social psychology, a concern of a later chapter of this book will be to explore tourist behaviour in relation to the environment.

This brief review of the geographer's concerns with tourism reveals that many areas of interest to the geographer are beyond the scope of this book. Thus the location of tourist activity on a spatial scale, and the concern with the overall design of tourist communities, will not be featured in the present analysis. However, when geographical interest turns to social class factors, the environmental setting in which tourists pursue their interests, and with tourist perceptions of their environment, then psychological research may be usefully employed to complement and expand on these topics.

FIG. 1.2   An example of strip-type development along a desirable beach-front environment (Surfers' Paradise, Queensland, Australia).

Anthropological studies of tourism

While economists writing on tourism concern themselves with concepts such as demand and supply, and geographers focus on locational analysis, anthropologists are to the fore in considering the human side of tourism. Anthropologists have been particularly concerned with the impact of tourists on the host community. When the people in the host nation are poor and technologically unsophisticated the advent of large numbers of tourists can generate discord, exploitation and social problems (cf. Smith, 1978a). A number of studies from around the world may be cited to substantiate this point of view.

Urbanowicz (1977, 1978) studying the impact of tourists from large cruise ships on the Pacific Island of Tonga notes that Tongan children beg from the visitors at major tourist attractions. In addition prostitution and homosexuality are seen as a response to the visits of the ships (both to serve the crew members and some tourists) while the quickly generated tourist dollars foster drunkenness and crime in the port towns.

Similarly, Mexican border towns have numerous prostitution bars for American tourists, while the Seychelles islands, promoted to tourists as "islands of love" because of their traditionally uninhibited sexual standards, now have "rampant" and "ferocious" rates of venereal disease (Turner and Ash, 1975).

Anthropologists have also noted that the simple process of tourists observing or watching the local people can have profound effects. Certain cultural and economic day-to-day activities of ethnic groups seem to appeal to tourists and are promoted in the media as tourist attractions. For example, Smith (1978b) demonstrates that tourists in Alaska frequently stroll along the beaches when local fishermen and hunters return to butcher their kill. Tourist expectations are fulfilled because the visitors are able to watch the "living culture". But the local people feel insulted, resent the constant tourist photographs, and tire of answering endless questions about their procedures. In short, tourists may destroy the privacy of the local people.

Further evidence indicates that the hosts may develop negative ethnic attitudes towards tourists. A study of the small Spanish Catalan community of Cape Lloc by Pi-Sunyer (1978) found that sterotypes of the numerous English, French, German, Italian, Portuguese and American tourists had developed. In common with other stereotype research, Pi-Sunyer establishes that while the original image may have held some "kernel of truth" with respect to a few tourists, in time the stereotype is automatically applied to all group members (cf. Campbell, 1967). Thus the Catalans see the French as pushy and bad-mannered, the Germans as stingy, the English as arrogant, and the Italians as untrustworthy.

For some small, technologically unsophisticated communities direct contact with tourists, if the latter come in small, manageable numbers, can be psychologically beneficial to the hosts. Boissevain (1979) notes that young people living on the Mediterranean island of Gozo welcome connections and friendships with tourists. They see such contacts as a chance to broaden their horizons and feel flattered that the visitors have chosen their island in preference to the larger more industrialized Malta. The sheer number of tourists visiting an area would seem to be an important factor affecting the outcome of direct tourist–host contact.

Anthropologists have also studied the effects of tourism on the material culture of the hosts. There is a strong view that tourism can provide social benefits to third world or technologically unsophisticated communities, by revitalizing ethnic arts and traditions. Thus Waters (1966) claims, somewhat eulogistically:

> This cultural renaissance is taking place all the way from the grass roots at the village level to the top councils of national governments. . . . With a modest amount of help, the native craftsman practising a dying art finds a new demand for his product and then employs young apprentices, thus teaching his trade to a new generation" (p. 116).

McKean (1978) studying Balinese society notes that the tourists' desire to view Balinese culture has led to what may be termed "cultural involution", the increased elaboration of established forms and practices. As a consequence, Balinese cultural expressions, such as wood-carvings, monkey-dances and dragon and witch displays, are now more widespread than they were a decade ago. Furthermore the dancing and craft skills are now included in the school curriculum. Similarly, Mackenzie (1977) discussing the "airport art" of Samoa, also suggests that certain local practices such as body tattooing are again increasing as a way of consciously expressing Samoan identity.

While ethnic art can be a source of local identity, self-esteem, and psychological satisfaction, it is not always seen as thriving under the influence of tourist interest. Graburn (1976) argues that tourists encourage a junk market of inexpensive souvenir art forms. While Navajo jewellery, Maori wood-carving and Kenyan face-masks are of undoubted quality and embody the best traditional skills, numerous wooden figures or paintings of Raquel Welch and John Wayne trivialize the local people's skills. This shift from the sacred to the profane in cultural crafts represents one instance of what Lambert has termed the coca-colonization of the world (Lambert, 1966).

One feature of selling local culture to the tourists is often overlooked. Many cultures attach enormous symbolic and spiritual importance to their ceremonies and art objects. Furthermore an adequate interpretation of these symbolic meanings may require considerable anthropological knowledge on the part of the consuming tourist. Without an understanding of the cosmological significance of cultural activities such as Aboriginal corroborees or Indonesian burials, tourists will merely see these events as "quaint" or "pretty" customs (Crystal, 1978; Pittock, 1967). This trivializes the local event and wastes an opportunity for greater cultural understanding.

While anthropologists clearly have much to offer in studying the hosts in the tourist–host contact situation they have tended to ignore the impact of the intercultural experiences on the tourists. Perhaps future writings will see an anthropological account of the tourists, noting tourists' rituals, group dynamics and the meaning of the travel experience. If this kind of work emerges it will usefully complement the work to be attempted in this volume where the focus of interest in tourism from a human point of view will shift from the hosts to the tourists themselves and their experiences, attitudes and motivations. Some of the concepts used to discuss the impact of tourism on the local people in the anthropological literature will be used in an attempt to understand the effects of contact on the tourists. For instance, concepts such as cultural involution, stereotyping and privacy will be used to account for tourist behaviour in the contact situations. As with the review of the literature on the geography of tourism this brief account of some themes in anthropology writing on travel suggests that a psychological account of tourists will provide a more complete account of tourism than presently exists. It is hoped that a psychological focus on the topic will address new questions and issues concerning the experiences of the tourists, rather than generating internecine arguments about the value of different approaches.

Sociological studies of tourism

Early sociological accounts of tourism tended to be descriptive and atheoretical. For example Forster (1964), by his own confession, deliberately avoided theoretical considerations in order to present his summarized impressions of the role of tourism in Pacific societies. His account, predominantly centred on Fiji, Hawaii and Samoa, demonstrated that tourism does indeed have profound sociological consequences by changing the distribution of the labour force, altering people's work habits and encouraging new forms of social stratification. In his concluding sentences outlining future research in the field of tourism, Forster observes "social psychological studies not only of changed attitudes, but of staging, setting and the presentation of self would be both interesting and useful" (Forster, 1964, p. 227).

Despite this early recognition for the need to provide sociological and social psychological accounts of tourist behaviour little systematic work emerged for almost a decade. There were some further descriptive sociological accounts, such as the volumes by Sandford and Law (1967), Rogers

(1968) and sections of the work of Turner and Ash (1975). These accounts do little more than mirror popular ideas about tourists. One of their chief functions seems to be to legitimize the process whereby one set of slightly more sophisticated tourists (those reading the sociologists's text) can laugh at and mock other tourists.

This kind of sociological criticism, which sees tourists as superficial devotees of synthetic fun, follows directly in the footsteps of earlier historical and cultural critiques such as those by Boorstin (1961).

Recently, however, sociologists have contributed more to an understanding of tourism than this rather shallow, overgeneralized appraisal of the tourists' culture and aesthetic limitations. For example, more precise attempts to understand how the tourist industry affects local self-esteem, job opportunities and social change have emerged. The work of deKadt (1976) and Finney and Watson (1977) has attempted to document these sociological roles of tourism. One example will suffice to give the flavour of this kind of work. It is often maintained that tourist development in an area changes the occupational possibilities inherent in the community. Kent (1977) argues that job substitution rather than job enrichment is the norm. He comments:

> For the working people of Hawaii, the widely acclaimed "age of abundance" has never materialised; tourism has only brought the same kinds of low paying menial, deadend jobs that have always been the lot of the local workers. The setting of a luxury hotel may be a world away from the sugar plantations, but in terms of the degradation and oppression of human labor, it is probably a good deal worse. (p. 182)

These views, while they contain something of the myth of the noble peasant toiling in the fields, are substantiated by the comments of the workers themselves, and Kent cites numerous quotations from the Hawaiian context to support his appraisal. The sense of oppression is not only confined to the workers, since even the more sanitary middle-class, management jobs tend to be allocated to foreign experts. These subtle forms of economic discrimination have profound sociological consequences and the development of local violence against tourism and tourists may well occupy the sociological accounts of tourism in future years (Matthews, 1977).

Sociologists have also been active in developing theoretical models and conceptual frameworks with which to examine tourism. These conceptual analyses attempt to explain both the reasons tourists travel and the nature of the tourists' travel experiences. For example Cohen and Taylor (1976), who draw upon Goffman's seminal concern with the presentation of self in everyday life, argue that holidays are culturally sanctioned escape routes for Western man. According to their view one of the problems for modern man is to establish an identity, a sense of personal individuality in the face of the large anomic forces of a technological world. Holidays provide a free area, a mental and physical escape from the most immediate reality pressures of the technological society. Thus holidays provide scope for the nurturance and cultivation of human identity. Cohen and Taylor argue that overseas holidays are structurally similar to pastimes, games and sex because one of their chief purposes is identity establishment and the cultivation of one's self-consciousness.

It is interesting that Cohen and Taylor do not simply view the tourists as innocents abroad imbibing whatever experiences are delivered to them. Instead they see the tourist as having to work at the problem of his identity which involves a constant appraisal of his satisfactions and dissatisfactions with his travel experiences and his larger role in life.

The authors argue that the tourist coping with his holiday uses the same kinds of role-distancing, self-awareness and accommodation-to-the-situation techniques normally used to cope with the boring reality of everyday existence. This interpretation has important implications for other sociological writing on tourism. It suggests that the tourist can see himself in a contrived, artificial tourist environment and distance himself from it by mocking it while briefly conforming to its demands. Furthermore, the tourist who visits such set-up environments as staged local ceremonies and dances does "benefit" in the quest to establish his identity. Such a traveller is able to use the fakeness of the situation to demonstrate his own perspicacity, he can compare his authentic experiences with the inauthentic and thus use all aspects of his holiday for the manipulation of his mental well-being.

Other sociological writers on tourism, without concerning themselves expressly with the identity issue, have also been concerned with the tourist's ability to understand his predicament when confronted with fake, synthetic "touristy" environments. MacCannell (1973, 1975) sees tourism as a modern functional substitute for the spiritual aspects of religion and argues that the many modern tourists are seeking authenticity and meaning. Their travels represent a journey to the sacred sites of our culture, the famous buildings, cities and favoured environments.

While this is still a very global analysis of tourist activity, it parallels Cohen and Taylor's approach by suggesting that the tourist is not distressed when confronted with an inauthentic display. MacCannell's analysis suggests that the tourist may not always see through the elaborately arranged staged presentation of naturalness, but this is not to argue that tourists want superficial contrived experiences. Interestingly when MacCannell describes the experiences of tourists who do see through the situation he suggests, like Cohen and Taylor, that these travellers are not shocked or angered by their insights. The very experience of inauthenticity is an experience to be woven into the fabric of understanding ourselves and other cultures. Recently E. Cohen (1979) has elaborated on MacCannell's description of different types of tourist space. Cohen sees four types of tourist space, as described in

Table 1.1. Cohen's appraisal of tourist environments offers many possibilities for research. It suggests studies where tourist establishments are classified into one of the four types mentioned. Next tourists could be questioned to see if their perceptions of the space accord with Cohen's predictions. Further discussion of this work will be included in a later chapter of this book where the sociological and psychological aspects of tourist environments will be explored more fully.

In the same paper in which he presents the model in Table 1.1 Cohen outlines a research strategy for a sociology of tourism. He suggests that future research should be processual (taking account of the time element in tourism's impact), contextual (considering the political equagraphical ecological circumstance of the study), comparative (providing analysis of several tourist situations) and emic (taking the perspective of the varied participants in the tourist situation).

While it is agreed that such research, if implemented, would boost the sophistication of studies in this field, it is surprising to note that the sociologists are still quite content to speculate on a number of central points, relevant to the understanding of tourism. For instance MacCannell's documentation of tourists' reactions to the various kinds of tourist space consists of no more than the anecdotes of a handful of informers, while the account of Cohen and Taylor is by their own admission dependent on "anecdotes, fictional accounts and personal observation". The need for social psychologists to map out and verify the interesting speculations of their sociological cousins is clear and insistent. It is appreciated of course that structuralists do not always admit the evidence of participants in contributing to the understanding of a phenomenon. But unless some point is worked out whereby evidence may be used to substantiate or reject a sociological perspective, then all accounts of tourists' experiences, motivations and perceptions of tourist space remain equally valid and hence inadequate. Three

TABLE 1.1   Types of tourist space (after Cohen, 1979)

	Tourists' impression of scene	
	Real	*Staged*
Nature of scene Real	**A** Authentic and recognized as such	**C** Suspicion of staging, authenticity questioned
Staged	**B** Failure to recognize contrived tourist space	**D** Recognized contrived tourist space

of the chapters of this book will attempt to explore the ideas of the sociologist with surveys, small-scale studies, inteviews with tourists and arguments derived from the psychological literature. These chapters will be concerned with the social side of the tourist, tourist motivation, and tourists' reaction to the visited environment.

There is a further set of issues in the sociological literature which need to be considered. The study of leisure has been a growing interest area of sociologists for some time (Veblen, 1899; Parker, 1975). Leisure research has developed its own definitions, theories and problems and often contains large-scale surveys on people's use of their free time (cf. Neulinger, 1974). Two theories accounting for leisure behaviour are widely quoted. These are the compensatory leisure hypothesis which argues that people seek the opposite kinds of stimulation in their leisure environment to that at work. Thus the bored, isolated production-line worker seeks the excitement of the pub, disco or cabaret while the over-stimulated public relations officer looks for quiet domestic weekends. The spillover leisure hypothesis suggests quite the opposite. Here it is proposed that the people seek the same kind of stimulation in their leisure environment as that found at work. The machine-paced industrial worker adopts passive leisure pursuits which are low in initiative and personal enterprise (e.g. TV-watching, sleeping), while the energetic professional has a wide social circle and skilled hobbies and interests to use his leisure time productively. These kinds of hypotheses about leisure–work relationships, while they no doubt need some refining for an individual's personal situation (Burch, 1969), might offer useful insights into the dynamics of travel motivation. The relationship between such general theories of leisure behaviour and travel behaviour will be explored, in part, in the next two chapters of this book. It should be noted though, that the leisure theories serve to describe people's activities in response to day-to-day work pressures. Travel behaviour may well prove to have several distinct and unique properties from that of other leisure behaviour because it may be seen as an infrequent, long-term and cumulative response to the work situation.

Other travel literature

Much other travel literature exists. There are anecdotal accounts of journeys by everyone from princes to eccentrics, from famous explorers to overgrown Boy Scouts. There is a standard weekly diet of newspaper articles on travel; fashion magazine articles on places to go; and a deluge of brochures and travel pamphlets. There are glossy journals produced by governmental tourist agencies and conservation groups, and private guides to eating, travelling and accommodation for every location remotely likely to attract the moden traveller. The chief factor uniting these publications is a sense of excitement. They manage to embroider the travel theme in a number of ways but above all that is said in the text the pictures convey the fact that the exploration of other places is potentially an exciting human experience.

In attempting a social psychological understanding of tourist behaviour it would be regrettable if something of this popular exitement and enthusiasm for travel were lost. It is of course a part of the understanding of science to uncover why tourists find travel exciting, but to ensure that this is not done in such a generalized abstract way that the individual tourist disappears. One later chapter of this book will deal with the travel accounts of individual tourists. Their travels will include a variety of destinations, levels of affluence and travel modes in an attempt to explore how adequately the earlier theoretical treatments cover the range of tourists' spontaneous accounts of their holidays.

Summary

In reviewing the major disciplines accounting for studies in tourism, several suggestions for developing a social psychological account of tourist behaviour have been made. These may be summarized as follows:

(1) A satisfactory experiential definition of the tourist must be developed. The economic studies of tourism provide a passport-type definition of international travellers but this fails to distinguish among such groups as businessmen, sportsmen and tourists. It is necessary to consider the social roles of the tourist and the feeling of being a tourist in articulating an experiential psychological definition of the tourists without neglecting the fact that tourists are also defined by the local community. An experiential definition of the tourist will need to reconcile the individual's own perception of his activity with the definitions being imposed by his hosts. The economic studies of tourism prompt an investigation of the social roles of the tourist in order to provide a clear account of what people do to define themselves, and be defined, as tourists.

(2) The economic studies of tourism also suggest the need to understand the differences among different tourist populations. This consists chiefly of categorizing tourists according to their motivation for travelling but may also involve considerations of socioeconomic well-being and on-site attitudes. One of the notable gaps in the existing literature on travel motivation is the failure to build on previous studies. A full consideration of travel motivation research in the context of the more recent psychological theories of motivation is necessary to provide a theoretical perspective and context in this rather fragmented field of enquiry.

(3) The geographical patterns of dispersion of tourist activity prompt questions concerning tourists' conformity and imitation of fashion. These

questions may again fit into the context of understanding motivational properties of tourists as well as drawing attention to the social class variable. The geographer's interest in environmental concerns directly relates to social psychological issues on tourist behaviour. It is important to establish the role of the tourists' immediate environmental setting in shaping behaviour. This in turn leads to environmental design questions such as the best ways to set up tourist viewing areas, as well as suggesting further social and environmental perception topics such as ways of establishing tourists' preference for scenery. Such variables as privacy, territoriality and cognitive mapping are relevant approaches to the theme of social psychological aspects of tourists' relationships to the environment.

(4) The social interaction between tourist and host is critical to the psychological understanding of tourist behaviour. While anthropologists have concerned themselves with the impact of contact on the hosts, there have been few accounts of the tourists' reactions to their contact experience. The extent of tourist stereotyping, culture shock, interaction difficulties and attitude change will be key topics to explore in accounting for tourists' social interaction. Questions of interest include the following: Under what contact circumstances do tourists come to like their hosts? Do tourists feel they are intruding on their hosts' privacy? What kinds of mistakes do tourists make while interacting with members of a different cultural group and how might these mistakes be avoided? While a global account of tourist–host cultural exchanges is beyond the scope of this volume, some specific studies and theoretical accounts of particular tourist–local contacts will be explored as a part of the social psychological account of tourist behaviour.

(5) The emphasis in a social psychological account of tourist behaviour should be on the findings of empirical studies. These studies may well include surveys, laboratory and field experiments as well as interviews, but it is necessary to approach the topic with systematic accounts of tourist behaviour to correct deficits inherent in the sociological literature. There is a good deal of interesting speculation and theoretical debate concerning the nature and quality of tourists' experiences but this is not always supported by high-quality and reliable evidence. Where issues and assumptions of a general psychological nature are involved, the evidence may not necessarily come from tourism-related studies. This emphasis on empirical evidence is not to deny the value of conceptual analysis nor the usefulness of anecdotal and personal accounts in capturing the richness of the complex tourist phenomena. But several of the arguments about tourists' desires for authentic and genuine experiences can be more profitably examined at this stage from the perspective of research evidence rather than by continuing with ideologically committed debate.

These plans and needs for a social psychological account of tourist behaviour lead to the following plan for this volume. In Chapter 2 the social role of the tourist will be examined in an attempt to provide a complex and psychologically adequate definition of the tourist. Chapter 3 will consider the motivation of the tourist both in historical context and in relation to current thinking in social motivation theory. These two groundwork chapters will provide basic definitions and categorizing procedures for a more refined and detailed appraisal of tourist behaviour. The detailed study of tourist behaviour will commence with a study of tourist–host social interaction. In particular the attitude of the tourist will be studied and the kinds of difficulties the tourist encounters in dealing with the local people will be highlighted. The tourists' attitudes and reactions to the visited environment will also be explored. These studies will encompass such topics as tourist evaluation of scenery, tourist behaviour in museums and tourists' use of maps to orientate themselves in a new environment. The richness and complexity of the tourist phenomena will be illustrated in a chapter detailing some travellers' accounts of their holidays. The usefulness of the previous research in explaining and examining these holiday accounts will be demonstrated. Finally, the closing chapter will summarize the current state of tourist research which has a psychological perspective and will seek to pinpoint key directions for future studies in this field.

References

ANDERSSEN, P. and COLBERG, R. (1973) Multivariate analysis in travel research: a tool for travel package design and market segmentation. *The Travel Research Association, Fourth Annual Conference Proceedings*, pp. 225–240.

ARBEL, A. and PIZAM, A. (1977) Some determinants of urban hotel location: the touristic inclinations. *Journal of Travel Research*, **15** (3), 18–22.

ARCHER, B. and OWEN, C. (1972) Towards a tourist regional multiplier. *Journal of Travel Research*, **11** (2), 9–13.

BLOMSTROM, R. L. (1967) *The Commercial Lodging Market.* American Hotel and Motel Association and School of Hotel, Restaurant and Institution Management Graduate School of Business Administration, Michigan State University, East Lansing, Michigan, 1967.

BOISSEVAIN, J. (1979) Impact of tourism on a dependent island: Gozo, Malta. *Annals of Tourism Research*, **6**, 76–90.

BOORSTIN, D. J. (1961) *The Image: A Guide to Pseudo-events in America.* New York: Harper & Row.

BRITISH TOURIST AUTHORITY (1972–80). *Research Newsletters.* London: British Tourist Authority.

BRITISH TOURIST AUTHORITY (1974). *Holiday Motivations Study.* London: British Tourist Authority.

BRYDEN, J. (1973). *Tourism and Development: A Case Study of the Commonwealth Caribbean.* New York: Cambridge University Press.

BURCH, W. R. (1969) The social circles of leisure: competing explanations. *Journal of Leisure Research*, **1**, 125–48.

BURKART, A. J. and MEDLIK, S. (1974). *Tourism.* London: Heinemann.

CAMPBELL, D. J. (1967) Stereotypes and the perception of group differences. *American Psychologist*, **22**, 817–29.

CHRISTALLER, W. (1964) *Some Considerations of Tourist Locations in Europe.* Papers Regional Science Association, **12**, 95–105.

COHEN, E. (1978) The impact of tourism on the physical environment. *Annals of Tourism Research*, **2**, 215–37.

COHEN, E. (1979) Rethinking the sociology of tourism. *Annals of Tourism Research*, **6**, 18–35.

COHEN, S. and TAYLOR, L. (1976) *Escape Attempts*. Harmondsworth: Penguin.

CORSI, T. E. and HARVEY, M. E. (1979) Changes in vacation travel in response to motor fuel shortages and higher prices. *Journal of Travel Research*, **17** (4), 7–11.

COSGROVE, I. and JACKSON, R. (1972) *The Geography of Recreation and Leisure*. London: Hutchinson.

CRYSTAL, E. (1978) Tourism in Toraja, Sulawesi, Indonesia. In SMITH, V. (ed.), *Hosts and Guests*. Oxford: Blackwell.

DEKADT, E. (1976) *Social and Cultural Aspects of Tourism*. Joint Unesco/World Bank Seminar on the Social and Cultural Impacts of Tourism, Washington, DC.

DUNN, M. C. *Landscape Evaluation Techniques: An Appraisal and Review of the Literature*. Working Paper No. 4: Centre for Urban and Regional Studies: University of Birmingham, 1974.

FERRARIO, F. F. (1979a) The evaluation of tourist resources: an applied methodology. Part 1. *Journal of Travel Research*, **17** (3), 18–22.

FERRARIO, F. F. (1979b) The evaluation of tourist resources: an applied methodology. Part 2. *Journal of Travel Research*, **17** (4), 24–30.

FINNEY, B. R. and WATSON, K. A. (1977) *A New Kind of Sugar*. Tourism in the Pacific. Santa Cruz, California; Center for South Pacific Studies.

FORSTER, J. (1964) The sociological consequences of tourism. *International Journal of Comparative Sociology*, **5**, 217–27.

GEARING, C. E., SWART, W. W. and VAR, T. (1974) Establishing a measure of touristic attractiveness. *Journal of Travel Research*, **12** (4), 1–8.

GILBERT, E. W. (1939) The growth of inland and seaside health resorts in England. *Scottish Geographical Magazine*, **55**, 16–35.

GILBERT, E. W. (1949) The growth of Brighton. *Geographical Journal*, **114**, 30–52.

GOODRICH, J. N. (1977a) Differences in perceived similarity of tourism regions: a spatial analysis. *Journal of Travel Research*, **16** (1), 10–13.

GOODRICH, J. N. (1977b) Benefits bundle analysis: an empirical study of international travellers. *Journal of Travel Research*, **16** (2), 6–9.

GRABURN, N. H. H. (ed.) *Ethnic and Tourist Arts: Cultural Expressions from the Fourth World*. Berkeley and Los Angeles: University of California Press.

HAWES, D. K. (1977) Psychographics are meaningful . . . not merely interesting. *Journal of Travel Research*, **15** (4), 1–7.

HUIZINGA, J. (1938) *Homo Ludens*. London: Paladin, 1970 (first published 1938).

HUNT, J. D. (1975) Image as a factor in tourism development. *Journal of Travel Research*, **13** (3), 1–7.

KENT, N. (1977) A new kind of sugar. In FINNEY, B. R. and WATSON, K. A. (eds), *A New Kind of Sugar*. Tourism in the Pacific. Center for South Pacific Studies, Santa Cruz, California.

KOESTLER, A. (1967) *The Ghost in the Machine*. London: Hutchinson.

LAMBERT, R. D. (1966) Some minor pathologies in the American presence in India. *Annals of the American Academy of Political and Social Sciences*, **368**, 157–170.

LEVI-STRAUSS, C. (1955) *Tristes Tropiques*. Harmondsworth: Penguin, 1976 (First published, 1955).

MACCANNELL, D. (1973) Staged authenticity: arrangements of social space in tourist settings. *The American Journal of Sociology*, **79** (3), 589–603.

MACCANNELL, D. (1976) *The Tourist*. New York: Schocken.

MACKENZIE, M. (1977) The deviant art of tourism: airport art. In FARRELL, B. (ed.), *The Social and Economic Impact of Tourism on Pacific Communities*. Santa Cruz: Center for South Pacific Studies, University of California.

MATTHEWS, H. G. (1977) Radicals and third world tourism: a Caribbean focus. *Annals of Tourism Research*, **5**, 20–9.

MAYO, E. (1975) Tourism and the national parks: a psychographic and attitudinal study. *Journal of Travel Research*, **14** (1), 14–18.

McKEAN, P. F. (1978) Economic dualism and cultural involution in Bali. In SMITH, V. (ed.), *Hosts and Guests*. Oxford: Blackwell.

NASH, D. (1979) The rise and fall of an aristocratic tourist culture—Nice: 1763–1936. *Annals of Tourism Research*, **6**, 61–75.

NEULINGER, J. (1974) *The Psychology of Leisure*. Springfield, Illinois: Charles C. Thomas.

PARKER, S. (1975) The sociology of leisure: progress and problems. *British Journal of Sociology*, **16** (2), 91–101.

PEARCE, D. G. (1978) Form and function in French resorts. *Annals of Tourism Research*, **5**, 142–56.

PI-SUNYER, O. (1978) Through native eyes: tourists and tourism in a Catalan maritime community. In SMITH, V. (ed.), *Hosts and Guests*. Oxford: Blackwell.

PITTOCK, A. B. (1967) Aborigines and the tourist industry. *Australian Quarterly*, **3**, 87–95.

RILEY and PALMER, J. (1976) Of attitudes and latitudes: a repertory grid study of perceptions of seaside resorts. In SLATER, P. (ed.), *Explorations of Intrapersonal Space*, vol. 1. London: Wiley.

ROBINSON, H. (1976) *A Geography of Tourism*. Plymouth, United Kingdom: MacDonald & Evans.

ROGERS, J. (1968) *Foreign Places: Foreign Faces*. Harmondsworth: Penguin Education.

SANDFORD, J. and LAW, R. (1967) *Synthetic Fun*. Harmondsworth: Penguin.

SCHEWE, C. D. and CALANTONE, R. J. (1978) Psychographic segmentation of tourists. *Journal of Travel Research*, **16** (3), 14–20.

SMAILES, A. E. (1953) *The Geography of Towns*. London: Hutchinson.

SMITH, V. L. (ed.) (1978a) *Hosts and Guests*. Oxford: Blackwell.

SMITH, V. L. (1978b) Eskimo tourism: micro-models and marginal men. In SMITH, V. L. (ed.), *Hosts and Guests*. Oxford: Blackwell.

SMITH, V. and WILDE, P. (1977) The multiplier impact of tourism in Western Tasmania. In MERCER, D. (ed.), *Leisure and Recreation in Australia*. Melbourne: Sorrett.

SOLOMON, P. J. and GEORGE, W. R. (1976) An empirical investigation of the effect of the energy crisis on tourism. *Journal of Travel Research*, **14** (3), 9–13.

SOLOMON, P. J. and GEORGE, W. R. (1977) The bicentennial traveler: a lifestyle analysis of the historian segment. *Journal of Travel Research*, **15** (3), 14–17.

THE TRAVEL RESEARCH ASSOCIATION (1972–80). *Conference Proceedings*. The Travel Research Association.

TURNER, L. and ASH, J. (1975) *The Golden Hordes*. London: Constable.

URBANOWICZ, C. (1977) Integrating tourism with other industries in Tonga. In FARRELL, B. (ed.), *The Social and Economic Impact of Tourism on Pacific Communities*. Santa Cruz: Center for South Pacific Studies, University of California.

URBANOWICZ, C. (1978) Tourism in Tonga: troubled times. In SMITH, V. (ed.), *Hosts and Guests*. Oxford: Blackwell.

VEBLEN, T. (1899) *The Theory of the Leisure Class*. New York: Macmillan.

WATERS, S. R. (1966) The American tourist. *Annals of the American Academy of Political and Social Science*, **368**, 109–18.

WATERS, S. R. (1980). *The Big Picture: Travel '80–'81, World Trends and Markets*. New York: ASTA Travel News.

WILLIAMS, A. J. and ZELINSKY, W. (1970) On some patterns in international tourist flows. *Economic Geography*, **46** (4), 549–67.

2

The Social Role of the Tourist

Introduction

The major disciplinary approach in this volume is that of social psychology. In employing a social psychological approach to tourists' roles and later topics, one must confront the issues that social psychology has many faces. Before 1970 questions concerning what kind of social psychological approach to adopt would have been relatively meaningless. Then, social psychology was conceived as a study of social influences on human behaviour, in short the effects of people on other people (Secord and Backman, 1964; Mann, 1969). The fundamental mode of examining these social influences was the use of a controlled laboratory experiment with its inherent logical positivist epistemology. While this tradition of research provided many insights into social behaviour in the limited context of the research room, questions of the wider relevance of research results emerged. These relevance questions led indirectly to a greater emphasis on field studies and experiments (Bickman and Henchy, 1972). The Humean notion of cause and effect persisted as the guiding theoretical framework of the field studies, but the range of situations and environments tackled provided some satisfaction for the critics who had complained of the irrelevance of the laboratory work.

The greater emphasis on situational and contextual determinants of individual behaviour and social behaviour sponsored in part the emergence of the related field of environmental psychology, which has often been seen as applied social psychology (Bell, Fisher and Loomis, 1978).

Criticisms of relevance and environmental context were not the only forces assailing laboratory-based social psychology. Other critical approaches, the effects of which are not yet fully realized, were also presented. A philosophical–linguistic attack, at times merged with a humanistic perspective, examined the very scientific foundation of social psychology (Koestler, 1967; Harré and Secord, 1972). According to these views social psychologists should move away from a search for facts and laws about social

26

behaviour and look for regularities and patterns in people's interpretation and organization of their social life. This was more than a simple shift in emphasis. It involved a shift from an etic to an emic perspective and a conception of the individual as a rule-using rather than a rule-governed, mechanistic, social being (Collett, 1977). These linguistic–philosophical criticisms which were essentially the product of European thinking can be juxtaposed with American concerns that social psychology is a male-dominated, Protestant, individualistic, ethnocentric and conservative pseudo-science (Gergen, 1978; Sampson, 1978).

The complexity and sophistication of these appraisals of social psychological enquiry prevent any single or simple solution. The resolution of having no solution, that is favouring a general eclecticism, is unacceptable because the approaches raise contradictory goals and aims. An exclusive reliance on one approach, for instance the conception of the individual as a rule-using agent, is equally inadequate since it considerably de-emphasizes biological determinants of behaviour. An approach favouring ethnological models of understanding will be restricted in scope, while complex cognitive attribution models may have little to say about the stream of everyday behaviour.

While a general solution, if there is one, to the question of how to conduct social psychological research is beyond the scope of this book, it is possible to choose approaches when one focuses on one particular topic such as tourist behaviour.

Studying the social behaviour of tourists presents some special problems. In turn, these problems limit the choice of social psychological approaches. For example, it is difficult to conceive of laboratory studies of tourist behaviour. Tourists belong in leisure environments, not laboratories. To lure tourists into the psychological laboratory, even overcoming the not inconsiderable problem that the tourists may not be too interested, severs the integrity of the person–environment relationship on which meaningful and natural tourists behaviour depends. As Tunnell (1977) has suggested, social psychologists should strive for three levels of naturalness in their research designs. There should be naturalness of behaviour, naturalness of the setting and naturalness of the treatment applied to the subjects. On all of these accounts laboratory-based approaches to tourist behaviour would be inadequate. However, as suggested in the first chapter, at times the findings of general laboratory-based studies in social psychology may be transferred, albeit with considerable caution, to the topic of tourist behaviour.

Another problem of tourist behaviour resides in its international and cross-cultural variability. This cross-cultural component of tourist experience necessitates a non-ethnocentric social psychology.* Yet again it is clear

---

* Our social psychological methodologies, whatever they are, need to be applicable across countries and across national, ethnic and racial boundaries. Where this is not possible, clear acknowledgement of the limitation of such procedures should be made.

that there are many views of tourists, both by observers and from the tourists themselves. A need to balance the emic and etic components of research into tourist behaviour is therefore a further necessity. Finally, leisure time, by definition, involves a degree of choice and control over one's behaviour. The notion that tourists exercise some control over their experiences and behaviour is consistent with the rule-generating model of social behaviour. However, there are writers who would argue that tourists are controlled and organized to a high degree (Boorstin, 1961; Schmidt, 1979) which is commensurate with a rule-governed notion of action. The interplay between these two interpretations of tourist behaviour and its consequences for social psychological enquiry in the area will be explored later in this chapter.

The ramifications of the above argument for the present book are considerable. In general terms the emphasis of the social psychological approach adopted will be towards a view of tourists which argues for a dramaturgical and self-determining account of behaviour. This will be integrated with cause–effect models of behaviour where it is clear that this Humean dichotomy is not a tautology. Such an epistemology will be used particularly in the realm of explaining tourist results from individual psychology research, such as the material on orientation and cognitive processes. An emphasis on the perspective and perceptions of tourists themselves as participants in the process of concern will be a recurring stance in the following studies. Ethological data, questionnaire and survey responses, unobtrusive measures, environmental analyses, naturalistic field studies and conceptual analyses will be favoured over laboratory and field experiments.

As discussed in Chapter 1, the major thrust of the present chapter will now be concerned with an adequate social psychological definition of the concept "tourist" and a demonstration of the usefulness of thinking about tourists in experiential terms.

Tourists and Others

The novelist Henry James had little difficulty in defining tourists socially. He decided that all tourists were "vulgar, vulgar, vulgar". Other definitions of tourism such as passport-type measures have already been discussed and their strengths and weaknesses outlined (cf. Frechtling, 1976, 1978; McIntosh, 1976; Chib, 1977). What is needed here is an account of tourists which seeks to delineate the tourist role from related roles. As Lengyel (1980) suggests:

> Tourists originally were a class apart. . . . Other sorts of travellers did not care to mix with them much nor were they necessarily obliged to do so. . . . Today, by contrast, travel for any purpose has become markedly homogenized: holiday-makers, participants at a professional con-

vention, archaeologists joining a dig, reporters covering an event, diplomats on missions and businessmen seeking markets are thrown together not only at airports, railway or bus terminals and in means of transport, but also often at the accommodation offered at their common points of destination. (p. 8)

It is useful here to summarize what is needed in a taxonomic appraisal of tourists' social roles. Such criteria can then be used to evaluate systematically the success of previous tourist role category schemes. These may be listed as follows:

(1) A broad range of tourist-related roles must be considered. (Range of roles)
(2) These roles need to be systematically separated from one another. (Role separation)
(3) At the same time as (2) above, it would be desirable to be able to express the degree of relatedness among all the roles. (Index of role relatedness)
(4) The process of separating tourist-related roles needs to be achieved through the use of experiential and social attributes of the travel experience. (Use of social/experiential criteria)

Table 2.1 provides an overview of some schemes in this area. It should be noted that the schemes included in the table refer principally to attempts which have tried to understand the broad spectrum of travel-related roles.

Cohen's 1974 classification of tourist roles, using fuzzy-set and multiple-criteria approaches, receives the most favourable assessment in the checklist evaluation of Table 2.1. There have not, however, been any further attempts in this direction.

The present author has extended Cohen's 1974 paper as follows. One hundred Australians who had just commenced tertiary education were asked for their perceptions of 15 tourist-related roles. These roles were chosen on the basis of previous tourist role studies and with a view to separating the tourist role from other roles measured by passport-type definitions. The people sampled had, on average, visited three overseas countries (the range being 0 to 79) and had explored their own country quite extensively (mean number of states visited 4, range 0–7). The sex ratio of the sample was approximately equal and the people had a mean age of 23·2, range 18–57.

The 15 tourist-related roles (e.g. migrant, traveller, explorer, jet-setter, anthropologist, hippie, etc.) were assessed on 20 dimensions or constructs. These descriptions of travel-related behaviours (e.g. takes photos, has language problems, contributes to the economy, seeks sensual pleasures) represent a summary of the main experiential and behavioural criteria employed in previous literature to define travel-related roles. However, as Cohen (1974) has argued, the applicability of some experiential criteria to tourist-

TABLE 2.1 *An evaluation of travel-related role schemes*

Author	Approach(es)	Basic elements of taxonomy	Evaluation on critical criteria for basic elements of taxonomy			
			Range of roles	Role separation	Index of role relatedness	Use of social/experiential criteria
Cohen (1972)	Defining criteria the degree of institutionalization and the impact on the host society	Organized mass tourist Individual mass tourist The explorer The drifter	Average	Good	Fair	Fair
Chadwick (1976)	Tree diagram	Pleasure and personal travellers Business travellers Migrants Students Crews Commuters Temporary Workers In-transit travellers	Fair	Fair	Good	Limited
Cohen (1974)	Fuzzy-set and multiple-criteria	Tourists Thermalists Students Pilgrims Old-country visitors Conventioneers Business travellers Tourist employers	Good	Fair/Good	Good	Fair
Packer (1974)	Synthesized from detailed observation of tourism in Greece	Tourist Jet-setter Corporation executive Back-packer Hippie Foreigner	Average	Fair	Fair	Average
Smith (1978)	Category	Ethnic tourism (tourists) Cultural tourism (tourists) Historical tourism (tourists) Environmental tourism (tourists) Recreational tourism (tourists)	Fair	Poor	Nil	Limited

related roles involves a set of category-related judgements which are best reflected in fuzzy-set terms of partial membership. That is, to define travel-related roles it is necessary to use a judgement process that permits degrees of membership of a role (e.g. businessman) to a construct (e.g. understands the local people). Fuzzy-set theory demands that a category (e.g. role) A can be defined by associating with each object (or construct) a number between 0 and 1 which represents the grade of membership in A.

In the study conducted by the author the 15 tourist-related roles were assessed on the 20 constructs according to a 5-point scale which permitted membership or applicability of a category to vary between 0 to 1. The useful-ness of this methodological innovation to tourist role assessment is twofold. On the one hand it enables a number of qualitative summaries within the sampling limitations of the study of travel-related roles by permitting a sys-tematic comparison of the constructs which define each role. Secondly, it permits the use of developments in fuzzy-set theory which offer quantitative indices of category fuzziness and permit the construction of a holistic view of the relatedness of all travel-related roles (Smithson, 1980).

The first view of the traveller-related roles is summarized in Table 2.2. In this table the five most typical (or least fuzzy) mean scores of role-related behaviour have been chosen. The five terms chosen reflect the mean responses from the 100 subjects on the 0–1 scale which are the most approp-riate to that role. Inspection of this table reveals in qualitative terms some of the major distinctions which travellers draw among these travel-related categories.

The information contained in Table 2.2 repays further attention. For example, it is interesting to note that the main distinctions between traveller and tourist perceived by the select sample used in the study lie in travellers being defined by the behaviours of exploring places privately and of experi-menting with local food. These items do not feature in the major definition of the tourist category. The holidaymaker, on the other hand, is charac-terized more clearly than the tourist by the dimensions of being alienated from the visited society yet contributing to that visited society's economy. The reader may inspect many other relationships and links among the role categories.

While this descriptive table offers a brief overview of the results of the study it glosses over some important details. The traveller-related roles are not equally well defined in that some roles are fuzzier than others. That is some roles receive more scores placing them along intermediate values of the 0–1 scale. It follows that the five clearest role-related behaviours for the 15 travellers' categories are not of an equal level of applicability to the role behaviour. For instance, the study revealed that the tourist role was defined by clear role-related behaviours. By way of contrast few of these behaviours were closely identified on the 0–1 scale with the overseas student category.

TABLE 2.2   *The five major role-related behaviours for 15 traveller categories*

Traveller category	The five clearest role-related behaviours (in order of relative importance)
Tourist	Takes photos, buys souvenirs, goes to famous places, stays briefly in one place, does not understand the local people
Traveller	Stays briefly in one place, experiments with local food, goes to famous places, takes photos, explores places privately
Holidaymaker	Takes photos, goes to famous places, is alienated from society, buys souvenirs, contributes to the visited economy
Jet-setter	Lives a life of luxury, concerned with social status, seeks sensual pleasures, prefers interacting with people of his/her own kind, goes to famous places
Businessman	Concerned with social status, contributes to the economy, does not take photos, prefers interacting with people of his/her own kind, lives a life luxury
Migrant	Has language problems, prefers interacting with people of his/her own kind, does not understand the local people, does not live a life of luxury, does not exploit the local people
Conservationist	Interested in the environment, does not buy souvenirs, does not exploit the local people, explores places privately, takes photos
Explorer	Explores places privately, interested in the environment, takes physical risks, does not buy souvenirs, keenly observes the visited society
Missionary	Does not buy souvenirs, searches for the meaning of life, does not live a life of luxury, does not seek sensual pleasures, keenly observes the visited society
Overseas student	Experiments with local food, does not exploit the local people, takes photos, keenly observes the visited society, takes physical risks
Anthropologist	Keenly observes the visited society, explores places privately, interested in the environment, does not buy souvenirs, takes photos
Hippie	Does not buy souvenirs, does not live a life of luxury, is not concerned with social status, does not take photos, does not contribute to the economy
International athlete	Is not alienated from own society, does not exploit the local people, does not understand the local people, explores places privately, searches for the meaning of life
Overseas journalist	Takes photos, keenly observes the visited society, goes to famous places, takes physical risks, explores places privately
Religious pilgrim	Searches for the meaning of life, does not live a life of luxury, is not concerned with social status, does not exploit the local people, does not buy souvenirs

Table 2.2 effectively ignores the overall clarity of the role categories and concentrates on the five best defining criteria. Thus, Table 2.2 is best interpreted as capturing the broad outline of the study rather than permitting detailed cross-category comparisons. Other techniques of data presentation will be used for comparative purposes.

Another perspective on the data set which offers additional information considers the 20 behaviour categories and lists in rank order the five most applicable traveller roles for each category. This information is presented in Table 2.3. This technique too does not consider the full range of the available material but it permits a more direct comparison of the relative behaviour-role links than does Table 2.2.

Inspection of Table 2.3 provides considerable information on how the 100 subjects related the traveller roles to the 20 behavioural criteria. The "tourist" category is featured amongst the five highest scores on 10 out of 20 role-related behaviours. The jet-setter category is placed 12 times in the five highest scores on the 20 roles while the traveller role emerged five times and the holidaymaker was featured on three occasions. These different incidences reflect the different extent to which traveller roles were given scores towards the 0 or 1 poles of the fuzzy coding scheme. It appears that people have a more extreme or clearer image of the jet-setter and the tourist than they do of the holidaymaker and the traveller.

It is possible however to be more precise in measuring the fuzziness of the 20 tourist roles than using the above rule-of-thumb technique. Smithson (1980) has developed a mathematical procedure to calculate the degree to which a category is fuzzy. In this context fuzziness may be defined as that property of categories or semantic units which permits graded membership. Thus fuzziness is distinct both from ambiguity, which may be seen in this framework as indecision between category placement, and from unreliability, which refers to inconsistent category assignment. The technique developed by Smithson permits a rank ordering of the perceived clarity of each role.

The results in Table 2.4 provide an empirical view of the fuzziness of travel-related roles. For each travel-related category one can see the degree of fuzziness which characterizes that category. It is apparent that the roles tourist, jet-setter and explorer are more clearly defined than the roles of traveller, overseas student and international athlete. This information does not provide an index of the interrelatedness of the traveller's roles but rather informs the clarity of each role in its own right. It may seem surprising that the tourist role is the least fuzzy or most clearly defined in the subjects' view of these 15 travel-related roles. There are two explanations for this relative clarity. First, the behaviours were specifically chosen to apply to the tourist role. They should therefore assist in defining that role clearly as compared to other travel roles. Second, there is no necessary correspondence between the difficulty researchers experience when trying to define a term such as tourist, and the clarity of that image in everyday usage. Indeed one of the strengths of the present approach is to remind researchers, as evidenced by the responses from the present group of people, that the tourist role has a well-defined "public image".

TABLE 2.3   *The five most applicable traveller categories for all 20 role-related behaviours*

Role-related behaviour	Traveller categories* (in order of importance)
Takes photos	Tourist, overseas journalist, holidaymaker, explorer, anthropologist
Exploits the local people	Conservationist (−), religious pilgrim (−), explorer (−), overseas student (−), businessman
Goes to famous places	Tourist, jet-setter, overseas journalist, holidaymaker, hippie (−)
Understands the local people	Tourist (−), migrant (−), jet-setter (−), anthropologist, international athlete (−)
Lives a life of luxury	Jet-setter, hippie (−), missionary (−), religious pilgrim (−), businessman
Keenly observes the visited society	Anthropologist, overseas journalist, explorer, missionary, conservationist
Interested in the environment	Conservationist, explorer, anthropologist, jet-setter (−), businessman (−)
Contributes to the economy	Businessman, hippie (−), tourist, religious pilgrim (−), holidaymaker
Never really belongs	Tourist, traveller, jet-setter, holidaymaker, overseas journalist
Takes physical risks	Explorer, businessman (−), jet-setter (−), overseas journalist, tourist (−)
Is alienated from own society	Hippie, migrant, missionary, religious pilgrim, explorer
Stays briefly in one place	Tourist, jet-setter, traveller, international athlete, explorer
Has language problems	Migrant, tourist, overseas student, international athlete, traveller
Experiments with local food	Overseas student, tourist, traveller, jet-setter, overseas journalist
Explores places privately	Explorer, anthropologist, conservationist, overseas journalist, traveller
Concerned with social status	Jet-setter, businessman, hippie (−), missionary (−), religious pilgrim (−)
Searches for the meaning of life	Missionary, religious pilgrim, hippie, anthropologist, conservationist
Seeks sensual pleasures	Jet-setter, missionary (−), hippie, religious pilgrim (−), businessman
Prefers interacting with people of his/her own kind	Jet-setter, migrant, businessman, hippie, international athlete
Buys souvenirs	Tourist, missionary (−), hippie (−), conservationist (−), explorer (−)

* A negative sign (−) after the traveller category implies that this traveller role is very low on the particular role-related behaviour. Though negatively related to this behaviour, the particular traveller category is in order of applicability ranked in the top five categories along this dimension.

TABLE 2.4   *Fuzzy-set indices for the 15 travel-related roles*

Role category	Fuzzy index (range 0 = non-fuzzy to 1 = totally fuzzy)
Tourist	0·46
Jet-setter	0·48
Explorer	0·48
Hippie	0·51
Businessman	0·52
Missionary	0·52
Anthropologist	0·55
Conservationist	0·55
Religious pilgrim	0·56
Holiday-maker	0.57
Migrant	0·57
Journalist	0·59
Traveller	0.60
Overseas student	0.60
International athlete	0.61

In order to fulfil the criteria for a good typology of tourist roles, as outlined earlier, it is necessary to interrelate the tourist roles in order to assess their similarity and differences. In the present study a multidimensional scaling analysis was carried out to provide an image of these interrelationships. The basis of this multidimensional scaling approach was a measure of association, obtained from the fuzzy-set analysis. This association measure, which is entitled the coefficient of synonymy, assesses the extent to which two variables covary away from a fixed zero point. It is thus unlike a correlation coefficient which assesses the degree of relationship between two variables as they deviate from the mean of each variable. It can be argued that when one is dealing with a data set which is concerned with the conceptual similarity of items, it is more meaningful to use an index which assesses synonymy rather than one concerned with mean deviation. The two-dimensional solution for the multidimensional scaling analysis was achieved with a low stress level (0·05) and thus provides a very good picture of the interrelationship of the 15 travel-related roles (Coxon *et al.*, 1977). The best way to interpret Figure 2.1 is to consider the distance between any pair of points as an index of their similarity.

Multidimensional scaling analyses can be "read" either by a dimensional interpretation or a cluster and regional interpretation. Since a good deal of information about the 15 roles has already been provided, and since there appear to be some clusters among the roles in Figure 2.1, the cluster interpretation will be favoured for this solution. Using the notion of inter-item distance in Figure 2.1 as a measure of conceptual relatedness, it is apparent that the analysis reveals a pattern among the roles which is readily

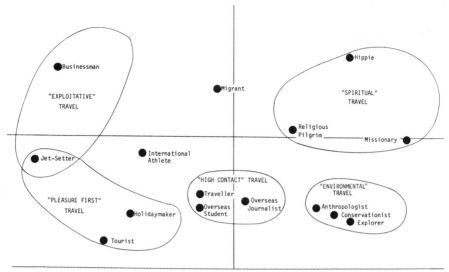

FIG. 2.1   A multidimensional scaling analysis of travel-related roles with suggested cluster interpretations (see text).

interpreted. The cluster of roles in the right-hand lower quandrant (anthropologist, conservationist and explorer) represent traveller roles with a socially and environmentally conscious, adventurous and professional character. The label "environmental" travel loosely summarizes these traveller roles. A second cluster of items if centred around the middle of the lower half of Figure 2.1 (overseas journalist, traveller, overseas student) and could be characterized as traveller roles involving considerable contact with the local people. A "high-contact" travel label summarizes this group. The holidaymaker role is seen as the closest to that of the tourist while the jet-setter role occupies a position between businessman and tourist. The position occupied by the tourist and the holidaymaker role may be seen in the context of the figure as emphasizing the transitory, exploitative, status-seeking, souvenir-oriented and safety-conscious components of these roles. The two labels, "exploitative" travel and "pleasure first" travel help characterize these clusters. In general the left-hand side of Figure 2.1 appears to be emphasizing the exploitative traveller roles, which are low on environmental consciousness and involve superficial host-guest interaction. The upper right-hand quadrant (hippie, religious pilgrim, missionaries) includes the roles which are not concerned with status considerations, which contribute little to the visited economy and which, in their separate ways, are orientated towards searching for some meaning to life. The description "spiritual" travel defines the common core component in these travelling roles. The migrant and international athlete are not readily integrated into the cluster interpretation but their respective locations in relation to the other clusters are broadly consistent.

The usefulness of this approach to traveller roles may be seen by relating previous literature to the multidimensional scaling figure. For example Boorstin (1961) has complained that tourists have destroyed the art of travelling. In his view tourists are passive, pleasure-seekers who have fleeting and insulated contact with the local people. Several of these ideas are borne out in the previous figure. The tourist–holidaymaker section of the quadrant was identified as emphasizing the transitory, exploitative, status-seeking, souvenir-oriented and safety components of travelling. However, as MacCannell (1973, 1976) has often suggested Boorstin's analysis is a little overdrawn. Other travel-related roles also contain some of these components. For instance the jet-setter and businessmen are exploitative and have little understanding of the visited people while the traveller and explorer have fleeting contact with the local people and are not at all integrated with the visited society. Furthermore it appears from the above figure that there is not the marked separation between tourist and traveller roles that Boorstin would have one believe.

Cohen (1972) has used the organizing principles of degree of institutionalization of the traveller role and the impact of the traveller on the host society to construct his category scheme of travellers. These criteria may be seen as unitary dimensions in the complex multidimensional space of Figure 2.1. For example one can hypothesize that a line drawn through the points of tourist, traveller, and hippie would neatly characterize Cohen's principle of degree of institutionalization. The second principle, the exploitative impact of the traveller on the host community, would serve as a good description of the x axis in Figure 2.1 with the jet-setter businessman and tourist roles leading highly on exploitation and the missionary, explorer and hippie having relatively low levels of host–society impact.

Overall, and within the limits of the sample studied, Figure 2.1 provides a view of traveller-related role which clarifies the complex interdependent nature of these categories. It will serve the useful purpose of acting as a reference point for what is meant in experiential and emic terms by the term "tourist" as compared to other travel-related roles in later sections of this book.

Some refinements to the tourist role

It can be suggested that some tourists provoke clearer images than others. For example Turner and Ash (1975) use unflattering photographs of aged overdressed westerners—in short the ugly Americans—to illustrate their study of tourists. Equally well-known images exist of the insular Englishmen on the Continent, of gauche young Australians in Europe, and sex-hungry Japanese males in Asia. All of these images, irrespective of their authenticity, fall within the range of the category of tourist but represent a considerable contrast of tourist behaviours and experiences.

In a follow-up study to the assessment of the relationships among traveller categories the author examined the effects of four factors in determining the character of the tourist role. The nationality of the tourist was considered to be important and was exemplified by a contrast between the images of Australian and Japanese tourists. A second important factor to be studied was that of age, which was operationalized as "younger" and "older" tourists. Thirdly, the type of travel arrangements used were considered. A contrast was made between tourists on package tours and those using individual transport arrangements. Finally, the destination of the tourist was dichotomized into two very broad categories; tourists travelling in their own country and those travelling abroad. These four factors when combined in all possible ways yielded 16 tourist types. (For example: young Australians travelling on a package tour in their own country.) These 16 tourist types together with the generic term "tourist" were rated by the same 100-person sample used in the previous study. Again the fuzzy-set measurement procedures were used and coefficients of synonymy scores were employed as input for the multidimensional scaling programme. The two-dimensional solution for this analysis was achieved with a very low stress level (0·00005) and thus provides an excellent account of the interrelationships of these tourist types. The central interest in Figure 2.2 focuses on the effects of the four variables in modifying the core tourist role. The relative higher coefficients of synonymy among these 16 points in Figure 2.2 (0·98) as compared with Figure 2.1 (0·95) (M. Whitney U-test 12·5; $p > 0·05$) also enables one to think of Figure 2.2 as a blown-up version of a part of the space of Figure 2.2 centred around the tourist role.

The most noteworthy feature of Figure 2.2 lies in the fundamental schism between those tourist types which involve travel abroad and those which involve travel in one's own country. According to the view of the 100 Australians sampled, tourists travelling abroad are much more likely to fit in with the core tourist role, which in Figure 2.2 is located on the far left of the two-dimensional plot. It is interesting to note that the abroad–own country division is more important than both the nationality and age of the tourist. The types of travel arrangements involved are also less important than the own country–abroad distinction in fostering the traditional "tourist" image.

Closer examination of Figure 2.2 reveals other consistent trends. The age of the tourists seems to be an important factor in contributing to the image. Throughout Figure 2.2 the older tourists, irrespective of whether they are Australians or Japanese, whether they are travelling abroad or travelling in their own country, and whether they travel on a package tour or by themselves, are consistently nearer the general tourist image than younger tourists of the equivalent category. Similarly package tourists tend to be closer to the core image of the tourist than do tourists travelling alone. This finding too is consistent across the various nationality, age and country-visited categories.

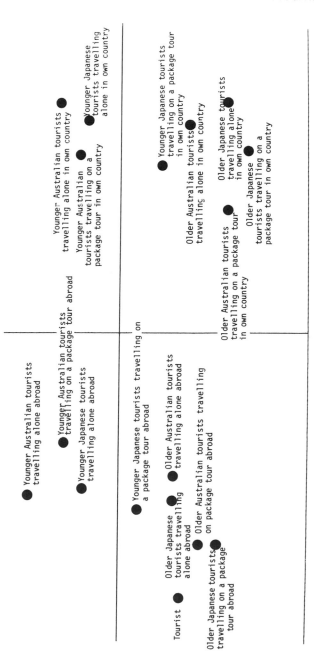

Fig. 2.2   A multidimensional scaling analysis of 16 tourist groups.

Interestingly the nationality category is the least important of the four categories and provides the most complicated cross-category interactions. If tourists are young, then Japanese tourists are closer to the core tourist role than are Australian tourists. However if these tourists are in the older category, then the nationality effects seem to be reversed. Older Australians are either closer or just as close to the core tourist role as their Japanese counterparts. It is quite conceivable that these results reflect the particular sample chosen through the operation of the twin factors of familiarity and role distance. The average age of the sample was 23, placing them within the broad category of younger Australians. Furthermore, even though Japanese tourists are relatively common in Australia, the people sampled are probably very familiar with the travel behaviour of their parents and older Australians. These two variables, familiarity and role distance, could well have led to an overemphasis of within-group differences between older Australians and younger Australians. Such an overemphasis avoids placing young Australians (cf. themselves) near the core tourist role which may have pejorative overtones. Meanwhile, the subjects' relative lack of familiarity with the Japanese and the lack of perceived threat or personal relevance in describing Japanese roles, may well have been reflected in the reduced levels of differentiation in the age variable when describing Japanese travellers. This argument is substantiated by a series of findings in more traditional social psychological research which has emphasized that more negative appraisals of out-groups occur because of more simplistic cognitive schema about these groups (Linville and Jones, 1980). These findings are also highly consistent with the notion of the self-serving bias in attribution theory (Kelley, 1971). As Forsyth (1980) argues, one can anticipate a self-serving attribution bias in those situations where the images and explanations of behaviour are ill-defined and ambiguous and where individuals or groups can cognitively manipulate the situation to create a favourable personal or in-group impression.

In combination the multidimensional scaling analysis of traveller and tourist roles permits one to think about tourists as participating in a special form of travel experience associated with transitory contact with a marked degree of environmental and personal exploitation. Further within the context of the traveller roles tourists are more concerned with status, souvenir-hunting, taking photographs and visiting famous places, yet rarely involve themselves in dangerous situations nor achieve much understanding of the local people. Within the tourist role itself a major distinction exists between tourists abroad and in their own country with important and consistent distinctions defining tourists of different age, mode of travel and to some extent nationality. The further use of these defining principles will be illustrated in later sections of this book.

An illustrative study of tourist roles

The usefulness of defining tourist roles from an experiential point of view will be illustrated here in a study of tourists' reactions to tropical islands (Pearce, 1981). The study samples older Australian tourists on package tours in their own country. A diary-based study of two tropical islands in the state of Queensland along Australia's Great Barrier Reef was undertaken with the aim of investigating changes in tourists' day-to-day moods. It was demonstrated in the context of this study that the visitors' changing view of their own role as tourists contributed to the mood fluctuations recorded in the study. This may be explained in more detail.

Each day the tourists were asked to fill in a two-page account of their holiday by answering a series of structured and open-ended items. The day-to-day record was divided into an activities section; a set of questions about the weather, the resort and its facilities; the number of people met; and a structured set of mood items for the morning, afternoon and evening of each day. The positive mood items used were relaxed, friendly, happy and peaceful. The negative mood items selected were frustrated, bored, tense and disappointed. These items had all been employed in previous adjective checklist studies of mood (McNair and Lorr, 1964; Raskin et al., 1969; Taub and Berger, 1974) and were used both because they were appropriate to the situation and because they sampled the range of moods found in previous studies.

Hinchinbrook and Brampton Islands, two popular and somewhat different holiday settings, were chosen for the study. Brampton is a large resort catering for up to 250 people with nightly entertainment. Hinchinbrook caters for about 50 people and offers little entertainment, but is actually built on national park property. This arrangement facilitates access to the unique environmental resources of one of Australia's largest island national parks.

The tourists were asked to fill in the diary for the first 6 days of their holiday. At Brampton Island 150 diaries were distributed over a 4-month period May–August 1978, while at Hinchinbrook Island, in order to allow for the smaller number of guests, 150 diaries were distributed from April to September 1978. The booking arrangements favoured by most tourist visiting these islands is a 7- or 10-day package tour from Melbourne, Sydney, Adelaide or Hobart (Southern visitors account for slightly under 50 per cent of the market) and 7-day package tours from Brisbane or other Queensland centres.

On Brampton Island 100 diaries were distributed with the instructions that the tourists should begin the diary on day 4 of their holiday. These instructions were directed towards obtaining a control group of tourist subjects who could be used to investigate reality and test sensitization effects which might be present in the diary format technique. As an incentive to all subjects, the researcher promised to return the questionnaire diary to the tourists after coding the responses for research purposes. Sixty-two fully completed diaries were obtained from Brampton in addition to 25 "control" group diaries. Fifty-three fully completed diaries were obtained from Hinchinbrook Island. In order to facilitate a precise and matched inter-island comparison in the following results, 48 tourist diaries were selected from each island such that in each case 24 of these diaries were completed by Queensland visitors and 24 were completed by Southern visitors. Southern visitors were defined as "non-Queensland" visitors. The percentage breakdown of the Southern visitors was very similar for both islands and overall was as follows: 41 per cent Victoria, 23 per cent New South Wales, 16 per cent Tasmania, 12 South Australia and 8 per cent from elsewhere in Australia.

The tourists sampled at both islands varied widely in age with a mean for Hinchinbrook being 42·5 (s.d.=17·6) and Brampton 43·7 (s.d.=18·6). Males were 46 per cent of the sample at Brampton and 42 per cent at Hinchinbrook. A wide variety of occupations was recorded, with the majority occupying upper to middle management and executive positions. A total of ten of the Queenslanders were farmers or farmers' wives. In checking the demographic characteristics of the sample with the island resort records of visitors, the only significant biases in the present sample were a slightly older sample of tourists at both resorts and a lack of repeat visitors to the islands. None of the tourists studied had been to the island before, although from the island records up to 10 per cent of the annual visitors have been to the specific island before. The occupational, state of origin, and sex characteristics of the sample approximate the characteristics of the regular clientele of the two islands. There were no important age, sex or occupational differences between the samples of the tourists on the two islands. Ninety-six tourist diaries were analysed in detail. Forty-eight completed diaries were selected from each island such that there were 24 Southern visitors and 24 Queensland visitors in both island samples. This marginal reduction in overall sample size (the total number of returned diaries being 113) considerably facilitated inter-island comparison in the graphs and results since a consistent problem emerged of finding data analysis techniques to handle repeated measures data of a non-parametric and often nominal level of measurement. The major patterns in the results can be readily appreciated in Figures 2.3 and 2.4 depicting negative moods in relation to the day of the tourists' visit. For both islands there were more negative moods experienced in the early days of the holiday. In particular the second and third day of the holiday resulted in a peaking of the tourists' negative moods which was followed by a steady decline of negative states throughout the rest of the holiday.

Since it was clear both from figures and corroborating analysis (Pearce, 1981) that the day of the tourists' visit was the major variable influencing

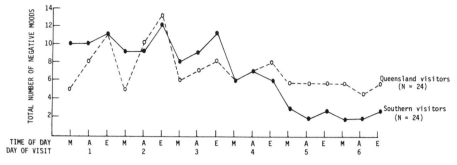

FIG. 2.3   Total negative moods as a function of the time of day and day of visit, Hinchinbrook Island ($N = 48$).

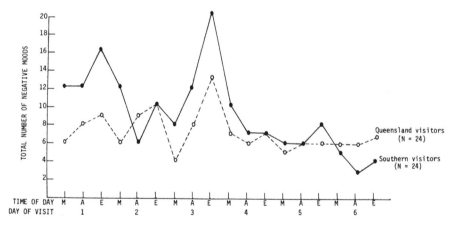

FIG. 2.4   Total negative moods as a function of the time of day and day of visit, Brampton Island ($N = 48$).

tourists' moods, it was necessary to explore this relationship further. A number of explanations were conveniently ruled out by the sampling procedures. It will be recalled that the tourists were not all assessed on the same day of week nor even in the same month of the year. Thus, such factors as indifferent weather and the weekly routine of the resort did not systematically covary with the tourists' day of visit. Furthermore, the number of people met by the tourists showed little variation across the 6 days. Again this factor appeared not to account for the mood dips and highs described earlier. However, the tourists' health reports and the tourists' activities and perceived role provided more fruitful insights.

The total data on the tourists' health were analysed using Friedman's two-way analysis of variance by ranks. The Friedman values and the patterns of health symptom differences totalled across both islands are presented in Table 2.5. Individual island analyses are not presented as the pattern of the results was very similar for both islands.

It is apparent from Table 2.5 and the Friedman analysis that the total number of both Southern and Queensland tourists' health problems varied according to the timing of the tourists' self-report scores. In particular it should be noted that the tourists (both Southerners and Queenslanders) report more health problems on days 1, 2 and 3 of their holiday than at either of the other two periods. A percentage comparison of the breakdown of types of health problems as reported in Table 2.5 indicated that tension symptoms decrease during the holiday, viral symptoms remain at about the same level and "environment shock" symptoms increase during the holiday period particularly for the Southern tourist. It is noteworthy that on days 4, 5 and 6 of the holiday tourists report a decrease in all health problems. This pattern of results lends support to the view that tourists' negative moods at the beginning of their holidays may be linked to the fact that they tend to experience some minor but novel health irritants during this period.

However, there is other evidence from the diaries which may also account for some of the negative moods experienced by both sets of tourists. It can be suggested that island resorts provide structured fun and entertainment for their guests. That is the island resorts tend to define the tourist role as one involving visitor participation in a number of structured activities. An examination of tourists' day-to-day activities at the resorts revealed an interesting trend away from such other-initiated or structure tourist activities towards self-initiated activities during the tourist's holidays (Figure 2.5).

Interestingly, the increase in self-initiated activities for both islands occurred on days 4 and 5. This timing corresponded with the tourists' recovery from the mood dip seen in Figures 2.3 and 2.4. It would appear, following MacCannell (1976), that many tourists tire of the structured "front-stage" experiences of the well-defined tourist role provided by the tourist resorts and may shift their behaviour so as to obtain "back-stage" experiences. In practice this role change meant more activities such as walks around the island, hunting for coral, flirting with new acquaintances, watching sunsets and reading, as well as participating in the organized fishing trips, entertainment nights and the disco–bingo scene. From Figure 2.5 it should be apparent that tourists did not refuse all structured activities, but rather that the relative proportion of such activities declined in relation to the total.

In summary this study of tourist moods on two Australian tropical islands reveals that the ways in which tourists and tourist organizers perceive the tourist role and activities will influence the quality of the tourist experience.

TABLE 2.5 *Mean number (and percentage in parentheses) of self-reported health problems by category prior to and during the tourists' holidays*

Component symptoms	Health category	Origin of visitor	Two weeks prior to holiday	Day 1, 2, 3 of holiday	Day 4, 5, 6 of holiday
Anxiety	Total	Southern	0·61	0·40	0·09
Headaches	"tension"		(36·3)	(20·7)	(7·9)
Migraine	symptoms	Queensland	0·52	0·36	0·21
Nerves/irritability			(33·1)	(20·9)	(9·8)
Colds/cough					
Nausea	Total	Southern	0·49	0·43	0·39
Stomach upset	"viral"		(29·1)	(22·2)	(33·6)
Vomiting	symptoms	Queensland	0·48	0·53	0·44
Diarrhoea			(30·6)	(30·8)	(35·8)
Constipation					
Ear complaints					
Skin rash					
Stings/bites					
Sunburn/sunstroke	Total	Southern	0·58	1·10	0·68
Excessive sweating	"environment		(34·5)	(57·0)	(58·6)
Tiredness	shock"	Queensland	0·57	0·83	0·67
Allergy	symptoms		(36·3)	(48·2)	(54·4)
Asthma					
Sinus					
Total health		Southern*	1·68	1·93	1·16
symptoms		Queensland†	1·57	1·72	1·23

* Friedman two-way analysis of variance by ranks $\chi^2 = 6·8$, d.f. $= 2$, $p < 0·05$.
† Friedman two way analysis of variance by ranks $\chi^2 = 6·1$, d.f. $= 2$, $p < 0·05$.

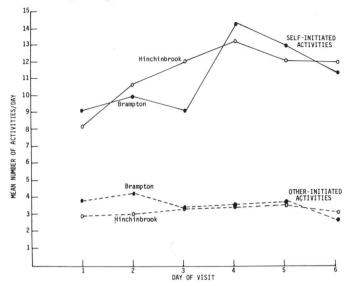

F<small>IG</small>. 2.5   The mean number of self-initiated and other-initiated activities as a function of the tourists' day of visit.

It also provides evidence that tourists from different parts of a country (in this case different states) will react differently to the scene provided or structured tourist opportunities. It is, for example, clear throughout this study that the Queensland tourists do not experience the health problems and do not change their activities and role as clearly as do the tourists from Southern states. It would appear to be profitable, therefore, to adopt these kinds of experiential definitions of tourists more frequently when researchers are enquiring into the quality and nature of the tourist experience.

References

B<small>ELL</small>, P., F<small>ISHER</small>, J. and L<small>OOMIS</small>, R. (1978) *Environmental Psychology*. London: Saunders.
B<small>ICKMAN</small>, L. and H<small>ENCHY</small>, T. (eds) (1972) *Beyond the Laboratory: Field Research in Social Psychology*. New York: McGraw-Hill.
B<small>OORSTIN</small>, D. (1962) *The Image*. New York: Atheneum.
C<small>HADWICK</small>, R. A. (1976) Some observations on proposed standard definitions and classifications for travel research. *The Travel Research Association, Seventh Annual Conference Proceedings*, pp. 81–4.
C<small>HIB</small>, S. N. (1977) Measurement of tourism. *Journal of Travel Research*, **16** (2), 22–5.
C<small>OHEN</small>, E. (1972) Toward a sociology of international tourism. *Social Research*, **39**, 164–82.
C<small>OHEN</small>, E. (1974) Who is a tourist? *Sociological Review*, **22** (4), 527–53.
C<small>OLLETT</small>, P. (ed.) (1977) *Social Rules and Social Behaviour*. Oxford: Blackwell.
C<small>OXON</small>, A. P. M., J<small>ONES</small>, C. L., M<small>UXWORTHY</small>, D. T. and P<small>RENTICE</small>, M. J. (1977) *The MDS(X) Series of Multidimensional Scaling Programs*. Edinburgh: University of Edinburgh Program Library Unit.
F<small>ORSYTH</small>, D. (1980). The functions of attributions. *Social Psychology Quarterly*, **43** (2), 184–9.

FRECHTLING, D. C. (1976) Proposed standard definitions and classifications for travel research. *The Travel Research Association, Seventh Annual Conference Proceedings*, p. 59–74.

FRECHTLING, D. C. (1978) A brief treatise on days and nights. *Journal of Travel Research*, **17** (2), 18–19.

GERGEN, K. (1978) Toward generative theory. *Journal of Personality and Social Psychology*, **36** (11), 1344–60.

HARRÉ, R. and SECORD, P. (1972) *The Explanation of Social Behaviour*. Oxford: Blackwell.

KELLEY, H. H. (1971) *Attribution in Social Interaction*. Morristown, N.J.: General Learning Press.

KOESTLER, A. (1967) *The Ghost in the Machine*. London: Hutchinson.

LENGYEL, P. (1980) Editorial. *International Social Science Journal*, **32** (1), 7–13.

LINVILLE, P. W. and JONES, E. E. (1980) Polarized appraisals of out-group members. *Journal of Personality and Social Psychology*, **38** (5), 689–703.

MACCANNELL, D. (1973) Staged authenticity: arrangements of social space in tourist settings. *The American Journal of Sociology*, **79** (3), 589–603.

MACCANNELL, D. (1976) *The tourist*. New York: Schocken.

MANN, L. (1969). *Social Psychology*. Sydney: Wiley.

MCINTOSH, R. W. (1976) Proposed standard definitions and classifications for travel research. *The Travel Research Association, Seventh Annual Conference Proceedings*, pp. 75–80.

MCNAIR, D. M. and LORR, M. (1964) An analysis of mood in neurotics. *Journal of Abnormal and Social Psychology*, **69**, 620.

PACKER, L. V. (1974) Tourism in the Small Community: A Cross-cultural Analysis of Developmental Change. Unpublished PhD dissertation. University of Oregon.

PEARCE, P. L. (1981) "Environmental shock": a study of tourists' reactions to two tropical islands. *Journal of Applied Social Psychology*, 1981. (In press).

RASKIN, A., SCHULTERBRANDT, J., REATIG, N. and RICE, C. E. (1969) Factors of psychopathology in interview, ward behaviour and self report ratings of hospitalized depressives. *Journal of Nervous and Mental Disease*, **148**, 87–98.

SAMPSON, E. E. (1978) Scientific paradigms and social values: wanted—a scientific revolution. *Journal of Personality and Social Psychology*, **36** (11), 1332–43.

SCHMIDT, C. J. (1979) The guided tour. *Urban Life*, **7** (4), 441–67.

SECORD, P. and BACKMAN, C. (1964) *Social Psychology*. New York: McGraw-Hill.

SMITH, V. (ed.) (1978) *Hosts and Guests*. Oxford: Blackwell.

SMITHSON, M. (1980) Notes on Fuzzy Set Analysis. Unpublished manuscript, Department of Behavioural Sciences, James Cook University.

TAUB, J. M. and BERGER, R. (1974) Diurnal variation in mood as asserted by self report and verbal content analysis. *Journal of Psychiatric Research*, **10**, 83–8.

TUNNELL, G. B. (1977) Three dimensions of naturalness: an expanded definition of field research. *Psychological Bulletin*, **84** (3), 426–37.

TURNER, L. and ASH, J. (1975) *The Golden Hordes*. London: Constable.

3

An Approach to Tourist Motivation

Introduction

A number of motivational explanations—some colourful, some speculative and some reflecting travel folklore—have been advanced to account for travel behaviour. Aldous Huxley (1925) wryly observed that "We read and travel not that we may broaden our minds, but that we may pleasantly forget they exist" (p. 12). John Steinbeck's comments on travel motivation reflect a prevailing view that travellers are affected by a pseudo-medical condition—"the travel bug". In *Travels with Charley* he observes:

> When I was very young and the urge to be some place else was on me, I was assured by mature people that maturity would cure this itch. When years described me as mature, the remedy prescribed was middle age. In middle age I was assured that greater age would calm my fever. . . . I fear that the disease is incurable. (p. 9)

There have also been warnings to those who would study travel motivation:

> Anyone concerned with the motivation of travel has to realise first that he is reaching deep into one of the major conflicts of the human mind: a desire for sameness, the return to the womb, if you wish; conflicting with the motivation to reach out and discover the world. In a sublimated fashion, a trip is therefore a form of birth or rebirth. Dichter (1967)

While the present chapter, hopefully, will be sensitive to the subtleties of the phenomenon of travel motivation, it will be argued that there are more useful and insightful approaches to the topic than this kind of psychoanalytic framework. Specifically, the present analysis of travel motivation will be undertaken by initially considering the trends of current psychological theory in the motivation field.

Subsequently, the motivations which have been suggested for travel behaviour will be considered; first by reviewing the historical forces which have shaped people's view of the purpose of travel, and secondly by a consideration of market research surveys assessing tourists' motives.

Additional consideration will be given to two recent integrative pieces concerned with the tourist motivation literature to provide specific motivational profiles for selected travel groups. The adequacy of these approaches to tourist motivation will be discussed and interpreted in the context of the preceding analysis of theoretical developments in the psychology of motivation.

Theories of motivation have played an important role in the development of psychology as a unique area of enquiry. In their separate ways, both the psychoanalytic theory of Freud and his followers and the drive reduction theories of Hull and the behaviourists, have emphasized the importance of understanding the forces which direct and underlie behaviour. These theoretical perspectives have also argued that everyday approaches to motivation are inadequate, since unconscious motivation and such behaviours as overeating and anorexia nervosa contradict commonly held assumptions about motivational influences on behaviour. There can be little argument that there have been some spectacular successes in explaining the causes of behaviour in clinical cases as well as in controlled laboratory studies (e.g. Arkes and Garske, 1977). Despite these successes, and the developments of other theoretical approaches to motivation (e.g. biological, instinctual, cognitive and self-actualization perspectives), there is a clear view that "motivation has been expected to and been used to explain too much" (Cofer and Appley, 1967, p. 837). The proposal that motivation theorists have been overly ambitious in their attempts to account for behaviour directs attention to the issue of "What is the role of a theory in motivation?" If one adopts the not uncommon position that all behaviour is motivated, then it is clear that the task of theories in motivation is to account for the entire range of human action. Psychoanalytic theory can be seen as consistent with this perspective, as it proposes that sexual and aggressive instincts are the root causes of all behaviour. An alternative view is that many behaviours are not strictly motivated but are the product of reflex actions, habits, and environmental and external forces. Such behaviours do not need to be accounted for in a motivational framework. Writers who adopt this second perspective see an advantage in re-defining motivation as being concerned with "energized" changes in the behavioural stream which characterizes human action (cf. Cofer and Appley, 1967; Arkes and Garske, 1977; Beck, 1978). This re-definition not only emphasizes a concern with the direction of behaviour but also highlights the consistent finding that motivated behaviour, at least in the early phases, involves the organism or person in increased levels of activity and arousal.

The emergence of numerous mini-theories of motivation would also seem to support the view that in the past motivation has been asked to explain too much. These more particularistic approaches attempt to understand energized changes in behaviour within specific contexts and for specific target populations. For example Roger's self-actualization theory deals with the growth and enhancement of an individual's self-concept. While self-actualization is viewed as a primary determinant of many human behaviours, it is clear that this theory is more focused in its attention to complex human values and aspirations than the grand-scale theories of Freud and Hull. Similar arguments of specificity might be advanced in relation to achievement motivation and attribution theory.

For the purposes of this book these developments in motivation theory offer several interesting possibilities. It is apparent that discussions of motivation are best conceived as applying to specific areas or domains of motivated behaviour. Secondly, focusing on a specific issue such as travel motivation enables one to develop a dialogue between the content area in question and the theories of motivation. That is, one is able to compare conceptual approaches according to their ease of use, thoroughness and insight. Such theoretical comparisons may possibly highlight some areas of the theory which need modification. These possibilities are consistent with the view, expressed earlier in this book, that the fields of tourist psychology and applied social psychology can form a useful symbiotic relationship through the creation of a two-way influence process.

For example, an adequate motivational account of tourist behaviour must deal with the same sorts of issues which confront motivation theorists in general. These issues include the question of the role of long-term motives, the question of who is explaining behaviour, the concrete problem of how to measure tourist motives, the possibility of multi-motive causes of behaviour and the topic of intrinsic motivation. These points, which are central to an appraisal of tourist motivation accounts in this chapter, warrant some amplification.

It can be argued that tourist behaviour is under long-term rather than short-term motivational control. It has been demonstrated that many tourists plan their travel months in advance, and while they enjoy the immediate satisfactions of their holiday, it is also apparent that there are long-term mental souvenirs and satisfactions which are enjoyed when the holiday is long since over (Clawson, 1963). As de Charms and Muir (1978) suggest, motivation must be conceived "as a function of how the task is related, in the life-space of the actor, to future events and possibilities". Achievement motivation approaches, particularly the work of Atkinson and Raynor (1975) have emphasized that motivation is related to the perceived success and incentive value of future tasks and outcomes. This emphasis on long-term incentives and rewards in relation to travel behaviour neatly reflects important conceptual issues in leisure research. In Chapter 1 the

compensatory and spillover hypotheses which relate work behaviour to leisure behaviour were outlined (cf. Wilensky, 1960). It was argued that one of
the enduring weaknesses in this formulation was the failure to consider
travel behaviour, and there may well be other leisure activities which fit this
mould, as a long-term behaviour contributing to the actor's work–leisure
relationships. It is likely that a more detailed investigation of the concept of
future orientation and long-term motivational goals and incentives from a
phenomenological perspective would add much to the contradictory leisure–work relationships debate. For the present, however, it is important to
bear in mind that tourist motivation must not be conceived as a simple short-
term process assessed by measuring the immediate satisfactions and causes
of travel behaviour.

A second issue in describing tourist motivation is concerned with who is
explaining tourist behaviour. Motivational accounts of tourist behaviour, in
common with other theoretical perspectives (e.g. perception attitudes) have
no ultimate recourse to the "correct" explanation of the phenomenon.
Accordingly, explanations and our investment in these explanations must be
tempered by the anticipated biases of observers versus actors, of tourist
researchers versus tourists, and of armchair speculators versus quantita-
tively minded data-gatherers. Fortunately sophisticated developments in
attribution theory provide a metatheoretical framework with which to
evaluate the motivational accounts of the above groups. Primarily one should
be alerted to the view that tourists themselves will be more likely to give
favourable explanations of their own behaviour, in terms of socially acceptable motives, than will tourist observers. This process will be illustrated in
later discussion of some of the schemes devised to assess tourists' reasons for
travelling.

The next problem area, namely that of measuring tourist motives, is a
familiar psychological issue in another context. The essential problem is
whether the data gathered is meant to have predictive value or whether it is
directed towards obtaining a *post-hoc* descriptive account of travel motivation. If prediction of some future behaviour is the aim, then questions concerning the precision of the prediction and its reliability emerge. If *post-hoc*
accounts of behaviour are at issue, there is an alarming tendency to be able to
bend any theoretical perspective to fit the observed outcome. Since it can be
justifiably claimed that these issues are not settled within the field of psychology itself, it is rather demanding to expect that they are satisfied in the context of tourist motivation. Clearly, though, there is a need to differentiate
between predictive and *post-hoc* accounts of tourist motivation and to consider seriously the breadth and reliability issues if one is concerned with prediction. The most useful guiding principle to follow in this respect might be
the attitudinal research of Fishbein and Ajzen (1974) who have chosen to
move in the direction of greater specificity of both action and situational con-

text in their attempt to predict behaviour. On the other hand a broad-ranging *post-hoc* account of travel motivation might benefit from summarizing across the specific situations and actions with the kind of generalized value orientation promoted by Rokeach (1968) and Feather (1975).

Another issue of concern in travel motivation is the notion that behaviour can be simultaneously motivated by several forces. Undoubtedly, the slow development of this perspective has in part been affected by consideration of parsimony; it has been rather too complex and confusing to contemplate the interactive role of multi-motive behaviour. However, some researchers, notably Atkinson and Birch (1970) have used achievement motivation and anxiety as two separate yet interacting motivations guiding behaviour. Similarly the attribution theorists in their emphasis on behavioural determinants such as luck, chance, effort and task difficulty (cf. Weiner, 1974), have contributed to the multi-causation of behaviour perspective. While this is not strictly parallel to a multi-motive development, it draws attention to behavioural determinants which do not stem from one simple single motivational source. This issue remains a problem both for an adequate account of tourist motivation and the development of motivation theories generally.

One further aspect of motivation which applies particularly to tourist behaviour necessitates attention; the question of intrinsic motivation. For many tourists and travel-writers the somewhat circular justification advanced to explain travelling is "to see the world". This expression is frequently considered to be an adequate justification of travel behaviour with no further explanations needed. This argument is closely akin to motivational enquiry in the areas of exploratory and curiosity behaviour where the concepts of intrinsic behaviour and the functional autonomy of certain behaviours have been outlined (cf. Allport, 1937). The concept that travel is intrinsically motivated is given tangential support by the entrepreneurial activity of certain businessmen who use free holidays and travel as a reward system in business organizations. However, whether the travel opportunities are inherently rewarding or provide scope to enjoy other activities is not clear in this instance.

The argument that travel is inherently or intrinsically rewarding does, however, need to be taken seriously, not merely because it is a common interpretation, but because it is linked with theoretical perspectives which remain unresolved in the motivational literature. De Charms and Muir (1978) argue that

> Intrinsic motivation presents a fascinating case of the "state of the art" . . . Sophisticated as we are in manipulating rewards and contingencies, we still do not know why or even if activities are engaged in for intrinsic reasons. (p. 107)

De Charms and Muir also suggest, following Csikszentmihalyi (1975), that intrinsic motivation offers the chance to study the experience of enjoyment:

> In these terms, the experience of enjoyment is not something to be explained away in terms of other conceptual categories but represents a psychological reality in its own right. An understanding of the structure of intrinsic motivation through a phenomenological account of the experience of enjoyment may provide the opportunity to re-conceptualise the epistemological framework in which motivation theories are traditionally cast. (p. 10)

Such an account might provide a non-deterministic view of human action which avoids prevailing reductionist approaches by emphasizing personal control and choice.

This possible development in motivational theories is consistent with the view of human behaviour and action advanced in the preceding chapter on the social roles of the tourist. It is not surprising therefore to note that in the writer's opinion a general motivational theory for tourist behaviour needs to fulfill this requirement of emphasizing the self-directing, autonomous, non-deterministic aspect of motivation.

To recapitulate, a motivational theory to serve the interests of understanding tourist behaviour needs to consider long-term goals, the perspective of the observer, multi-motive causes of behaviour, measurement issues and the qualitatively different non-deterministic nature of intrinsically motivated behaviours. It can be argued that while no single prevailing theory of motivation fits all these requirements, a combination of Maslow's hierarchy model, and some features of attribution theory and achievement motivation, will serve as an interlocking set of ideas which should be considered in accounting for tourist motivation.

The use of Maslow's theory as a basic framework is appealing on two grounds. First it provides a comprehensive coverage of human needs organized into a hierarchical framework which is based on the immediacy of the needs. Second the concept of self-actualization, as defined by Maslow, contains an inherent notion of individual choice and self-determination. This emphasis is consistent, as suggested before, with the view that some part of an adequate tourist motivational theory must be devoted to the non-deterministic nature of intrinsically motivated behaviour. This is not to suggest that studying this type of motivation is impossible or inappropriate, but rather that it requires a more descriptive, sensitive, emic framework than is normally applied in motivational theory. Maslow's approach alone is, however, not enough. The additional notions of actor–observer differences in accounting for behaviour need to be recruited from attribution theory, particularly as these proposals address important issues in measurement and actor–observer differences. The value of adding insights from achievement motivation lies particularly in the area of long-term goals and their role in accounting for present behaviour. Without this insight one would be left with a tourist motivation framework which was rooted to the present and ignored the teleological implications of current behaviours.

These ideas will provide our intellectual baggage in the journey through the tourist motivation literature. Obviously other insights could be added from learning theory and psychoanalytic theory but it is necessary to limit the luggage to an economical and hopefully elegant central core.

Three major types of tourist motivation literature may be distinguished. There are a number of historical, macrosociological account of tourists' reasons for travelling which summarize major travel determinants across the centuries. Second, there is a set of specific market research approaches which attempt to predict or identify the motives of specific tourists in specific contexts. Finally, there have been some recent integrative pieces which have attempted to follow the more general psychological approach outlined in this chapter. Each of these areas will be considered in relation to the theoretical arguments outlined above.

Historical approaches to travel motivation

Wolfe (1967) points out that most of the wealthier members of Alexandrian, Athenian and Roman society owned summer resorts which they frequented annually. Apparently, the principal purpose of these holidays was to escape the stifling heat of the main cities. The journeys to these summer resorts, which were often located in the mountains, soon became an important part of the holiday itself since various resting points along the route became centres of social activity. The Romans in particular seem to have travelled considerable distances for such relaxation, thus enhancing both their knowledge of the Empire and their social contacts (cf. Pliny, 1966). The Romans were particularly successful in creating a politically stable world, at least in Europe, and accordingly the Roman traveller had virtually unlimited territories to explore (Casson, 1974). For example the adventurous Roman could make his way from the Euphrates to Hadrian's wall needing only one set of currency and two languages for the whole trip; an impressive achievement even by twentieth-century standards.

However, if political stability is one prerequisite for leisure travel, affluence is another. The Roman citizen was the beneficiary of the vast wealth of the distant occupied countries and this gave the individual traveller great mobility and purchasing power. The Romans too can rightly be regarded as the world's first souvenir-hunters. According to Casson, popular items were paintings by the great masters, the mutilated limbs of saints, and Asian silks. Often it appears that souvenir-hunting was a major function of travel for the civilized Roman and the domestic ornaments discovered in archaeological digs often have distant origins (Anthony, 1973).

In the Middle Ages a new seriousness in travel motivation related to the emergence of the pilgrimage can be discerned. The original pilgrimages were essentially journeys to sacred places undertaken because of religious motives. According to Hill (1965):

> The fundamental conception is always in the idea that the deity resides or exercises some peculiarly powerful influence in some definite locality, and to this locality the devout repair either in reverence to their God or in quest of his assistance or bounty. (p. 5)

Over time the nature of the pilgrimage changed. Revelry and feasting became important accompaniments to the journey and ancillary services were set up to cater for pilgrims and their reputed "licentious living" (Rowling, 1971). Many pilgrims, like modern travellers, collected items to demonstrate their achievements. Appraising these collections seven centuries later, Mark Twain (1869) wryly remarked:

> We find a piece of the true cross in every old church we go into and some of the nails that held it together. I would not like to be positive but I think we have seen as much as a keg of these nails. (p. 108)

The legacy of the pilgrimage for modern travel is three-fold. It created a definite sublime goal at the end of the journey, a feature which was not apparent in ancient travel. Furthermore the essentially spiritual, non-secular nature of the pilgrimage elevated the importance attached to travelling in an individual's life. For example, to make a pilgrimage to the Holy Land became one of the major events in one's life. Finally the collector mentality which was noted in the classical era was strongly reinforced by the pilgrim's desire to demonstrate in concrete terms that his journey had been successful.

Another major development in the historical reasons for travelling can be seen in the emergence of the "Grand Tour". Intended principally as a training ground for the young and wealthy members of Elizabeth I's court, the tour was designed to "unite the knowledge of a scholar with the manners of a courtier" (Hibbert, 1969). The grand "Tourist"—the word was first used by Lassels in 1670—was typically the elder son of an aristocratic family with the time and affluence to afford a 2–3-year excursion. The young gentleman, usually less than 20 and sometimes as young as 14, was accompanied by a tutor who supervised his moral development and a servant who attended to more menial matters.

Initially, the tours were rather flippant adventures, but by the end of the eighteenth century the practice had gained favour as an ideal finishing school for a youth's education. This educational aspect of the tourist's experience is illustrated by Hibbert's comment:

The tourist must always be asking questions—one book makes one hundred and seventeen suggestions for those without natural curiosity—questions about the pay of the clergy, military training, funeral arrangements, grounds for divorce, water supplies, fire precautions, corporal punishment at the university or the care of paupers in the workhouse. And having discovered the answers to his questions, he must write them down in his notebook. (p. 20)

The merits of the tour as an educational experience were sometimes called into question. Adam Smith (1775) complained that the tourist returned home

more conceited, more unprincipled, more dissipated and more incapable of any serious application either to study or to business, than he could well have become in so short a time had he lived at home. (In Hibbert (1969) p. 224)

It was, however, the affectation of the tourist which received the most striking comment. Parents complained that they could no longer understand the vocabulary or mannerisms of their sons. Those tourists who imitated Italian fashions received the title of "Macaroni". The *Oxford Magazine* epitomizes, in its comments, the negative view of the returning tourist. In June 1770, the editorial observed:

There is indeed a kind of animal, neither male nor female, a thing of the neuter gender, lately started up amongst us. It is called a Macaroni. It talks without meaning, it smiles without pleasantry, it rides without exercise, it wenches without passion. (In Hibbert (1969) p. 234)

Three major forces brought the Grand Tour to the end of its own journey. The Napoleonic Wars effectively stopped travel in Europe for 30 years, thus creating a break in the tradition. The increasing affluence of Britain generated a wealthier middle class who were eager to travel abroad, and by the end of the wars could do so. And finally the revolutionary effect of the railway was important since it created overland mass transport possibilities hitherto unknown (Pudney, 1954).

In the nineteenth century, the rise of the famous spas and sea resorts throughout England and Europe lent another purpose to travel (Granville, 1841). Now travel and tourism became associated with health and, in turn, with rest and relaxation. The phenomenal importance of the railway in affecting this popular change has been strongly emphasized (Pudney, 1954; Swinglehurst, 1974), and indeed the residual pattern of this transport system, and its attendant hotels, may still be found throughout Europe today (Cosgrove and Jackson, 1972).

Two more developments of the nineteenth century which altered the history of tourism and the motivation to travel should be mentioned. The first concerns the emergence of shrewd entrepreneurs like Thomas Cook, who both organized and supervised tourist groups. Cook and his army of men led tourist groups to Europe and the Middle East and his influence in making travel accessible to large numbers of people was enormous. The second contribution of the nineteenth century to the history of travel was an increased awareness of the beauty of the natural world. The formation of national parks and the commercial development of areas of great natural beauty throughout the nineteenth century can properly be seen as the foundations of "environmental tourism" (Ittleson *et al.*, 1974; Smith, 1978). The Romantic movement in English poetry may be seen as an elegant expression of this change of attitude to the natural environment.

The nineteenth-century patterns of tourist activity persisted until the First World War. After 1918 several social and economic changes took place which were to have a powerful effect upon travel. The pertinent changes included regular paid holidays for everyone, the increased popularity of the automobile and the building of huge ocean-going liners for intercontinental travel. The car increased the flexibility and the range of the traveller enormously (Burkart and Medlik, 1974), while the passenger ship was a big success with the wealthy. Seaside camps were set up for those still not able to afford overseas travel and the popularity of sea resorts in general continued to rise (Brunner, 1945).

After the Second World War two new forces combined to reshape overseas travel. Much had been learnt about air transport during the war and its possibilities as a mass transport system slowly became apparent. Meanwhile hotel-owners along the Mediterranean began to treat tourism as an industry. Economic principles, such as economies of scale, were soon recognized. The merging of these two forces in the late 1950s produced the growth of the package tour; a concept which meant cheaper travel for more people and increased profits for airline and hotel operators (Young, 1973).

The magnitude of the travel phenomenon in the twentieth century is illustrated by the now dated but still relevant comment of Pimlott (1947) who summarized the situation as follows:

> in the present century holidays have become a cult. . . . For many they are the principal objects for life—saved and planned for during the rest of the year and enjoyed in retrospect when they are over. (p. 211)

The traditional pattern of visiting only certain European countries has been largely shattered and tourism is now a worldwide phenomenon. Aldous Huxley in 1925 commented that his children would have to take their holidays in central Asia, a suggestion which materialized in the so-called "hippie trail" to Katmandu (Alderson, 1971; Neville, 1971). Dulles (1966) observed

that Americans in particular have been influential in fostering the development of non-European tourist destinations, especially in their influence on
the Caribbean and the Pacific. But as Burkart and Medlik (1974) point out,
the Mediterranean countries still exert a major attraction for northern European tourists. The range of motivations suggested, and the somewhat
superficial level which characterizes any historical summary of travel motivation, prevents any simple application of the combined hierarchy–attribution–achievement motivation perspective outlined earlier. Nevertheless,
the chief motivations which were identified in the historical review—namely
travel for health, education, spiritual values and self-indulgence—can be
related quite well to the principles of the combined theoretical framework.
For example travelling for health reasons corresponds to concerns with
emotional and physical security, educational travel may be related to self-
esteem needs, a quest for spiritual values has close links with the search for
self-actualization, and self-indulgent travel motives may be linked with the
satisfaction of physiological needs and some love and belongingness needs.

One particularly useful feature of the historical review of travel motivation lies in drawing attention to the kinds of retrospective social comparisons
which tourists may use in defining their travel purposes. For example some
travellers may enjoy cruises of the Nile because of the direct comparisons
they may be able to make between their own behaviour and that of Thomas
Cook's nineteenth-century travel groups. This notion of retrospective social
comparison as applied to motivation suggests that motives such as self-
esteem and achievement may not only be linked to the rewards of the present activity and its future outcomes but may be specifically related to perceived images of the past.

Contemporary approaches to travel motivation

From the above discussion it is readily apparent that considerable sensitivity
and a host of motivational issues need to be considered to provide a
thorough account of the travel motivations of any sub-group of tourists.
While the current psychological perspective can be related to broad-scale
historical summaries of travel behaviour it is more directly relevant to contemporary travel motivation in well-defined sub-groups of travellers.

A typical travel motivation study as reported in the professional and governmental tourist literature will be evaluated according to these criteria. In
seeking the strengths and weaknesses of this kind of research it is only fair to
point out that the aims of the research pieces may be quite specific, and may
be seeking only particular kinds of motivational information.

A characteristic piece of motivational research of some subtlety and complexity is provided by the 1970 Canadian Motivation to Travel and Vacations study (Canadian Government Travel Bureau, 1972). This study used a

group discussion and interviewing technique to obtain people's perceived travel motivations.

Advertising films and travelogues were used as a basis to stimulate group discussion, and a total of over 5000 Canadians from 10 Canadian cities participated in the 30–50-person group discussion evenings. This technique of eliciting motivational information in general discussion was supplemented by market research personnel asking some specific questions of the group participants. The sessions were tape-recorded. It is worth considering this approach a little further as it has also been used extensively by numerous American market research teams as well as bodies such as the British Tourist Authority and The Australian Tourist Commission. From a sampling point of view, this procedure offers the possibility of large numbers of systematically selected discussion participants. It therefore permits the data to be analyzed in terms of age, sex, demographic and regional biases. However, there are two sources of misgiving about the quality of the obtained data. The group testing situation involves a degree of measurement reactivity which might be producing highly conformist responses. For instance, it is unlikely that many people would advance deeply personal or intimate reasons for travelling in this situation, but might be quite prepared to agree with socially desirable motives such as travelling for cultural enlightenment. In addition the format in which the motives are cast emphasizes the attractions or the features of the destination (e.g. relaxing atmosphere, night-life). This emphasis ignores the psychological intra-personal needs of the travellers and instead provides a profile of perceived destination attractiveness. Despite these concerns, the large samples and thorough reporting of the data offer some insights for those concerned with travel motivation. An example of the data obtained is provided in Table 3.1 which features the responses to an open-ended question seeking *all* reasons for the choice of destination.

In Table 3.1 the importance of visiting friends or relations of finding a relaxing atmosphere and of seeking a good climate with beautiful scenery are emphasized in the Canadian vacationers' choice of destinations.

Furthermore, considerable differences between holiday destinations emerge particularly along certain key dimensions such as weather (e.g. Britain 7 per cent, Mexico, Caribbean and Central America 76 per cent), night-life (Canada 5 per cent, Mexico, Caribbean and Central America 28 per cent), and oceans and beaches (South-East U.S.A. 57 per cent, Total Europe 11 per cent). For its purposes, therefore, this kind of study provides important marketing information highlighting the perceived images of different holiday areas according to the demographic characteristics of the potential consumer. However, such an approach barely relates to the kind of motivational theories to account for tourist behaviour discussed earlier in this chapter. The key feature which is missing in this kind of study from a

TABLE 3.1   *Canadian vacation travellers: all reasons for choosing last vacation destination (percentages)*

All reasons for destination choice	All destinations	Total Canadian	Total U.S.A.	Mid-Atlantic region	New England region	North Central	North-West	South-West	South-East/Central	U.S.A. (State unspecified)	Total other countries	Total Europe	British Isles	Other Europe	Mexico, Bermuda, Caribbean, Central and South America	All other destinations
To visit friends or relatives	50	53	39	37	37	63	40	53	21	35	59	73	78	71	29	34
Relaxing atmosphere	33	33	31	28	37	18	35	29	41	25	32	22	28	18	62	38
Scenery	41	43	35	30	40	26	29	40	39	38	40	33	34	33	52	55
For oceans and beaches	19	15	33	29	49	4	19	19	57	33	22	11	7	14	57	24
Sports facilities	10	11	8	5	8	9	9	6	12	7	3	1	—	2	8	7
Good camp-sites	11	13	10	7	11	9	10	4	8	19	*	*	1	—	—	2
Good weather there	24	20	37	27	36	15	15	50	68	37	33	18	7	24	76	42
Not too many tourists	10	11	6	5	11	4	5	1	3	7	6	4	6	3	8	13
To get better buys	4	2	9	9	8	15	19	10	5	6	7	8	7	8	2	6
Low cost of vacations	11	12	8	5	8	7	8	11	7	8	11	8	8	8	17	16
Warm, friendly people	22	21	22	20	23	24	20	25	26	20	33	36	38	35	25	30
Good roads	13	13	18	19	16	14	12	15	17	24	1	1	1	*	1	—
Outstanding food	7	6	5	4	2	5	7	5	5	7	16	14	6	19	22	17
Attractive customs, life	7	5	7	9	7	3	5	12	4	9	23	21	21	21	24	34
Foreignness	7	4	13	17	14	7	8	17	14	11	22	19	13	22	22	39
Night-life	6	5	10	13	4	15	5	14	13	5	13	8	5	9	28	19
Easier to have fun there	13	13	10	16	8	6	4	15	9	10	12	8	7	9	22	18
Cultural activities	5	4	5	5	5	2	10	—	8	3	14	15	18	13	4	26
Attractive advertising	5	4	9	15	8	1	2	8	13	7	7	3	2	4	15	14
Don't know much about own province's attractions	2	2	2	4	*	1	—	1	4	1	1	1	—	1	1	4
Don't make fun of English	3	2	5	10	6	2	1	1	8	4	2	1	1	2	6	1
Kicks of getting something back through customs	1	*	3	6	2	1	8	4	3	1	1	1	1	1	—	4
None of above	9	9	7	6	6	7	4	7	5	15	5	6	6	6	3	2

* Less than 1 per cent.
Source: Canadian Government Travel Bureau, 1972.

psychological perspective is a proper account of what travel means to each participant. For example, the presence of oceans and beaches might be attractive to tourists for different reasons. For one group the surf and sand may represent entertainment for children; for another group the coast provides a venue for social and possibly sexual encounters. This difference matters, both from a theoretical and marketing perspective.

Without some attention to these individual motivational perspectives it is hard to justify the claim that these reports are "motivational" studies when in fact they read as interesting comparisons of destination images. According to the motivational perspective adopted in this chapter many of the professional and governmental accounts of travel motivation should be re-classified with the geographical material discussed in Chapter 1, which is concerned with destination resources and images.

Large-scale market research studies of tourist motivation exist side by side with smaller more intensive motivational profiles of particular travel sub-groups. Again a relatively typical study of this genre will be considered. The study in question is that of Solomon and George (1977) who analysed questionnaire reponses from 162 car-travellers to the U.S. state of Virginia. The researchers were concerned with two travel groups: those who expressed an interest in historical places and events ("historians"), and those not particularly interested in the historical associations of visited places (non-historians). Solomon and George demonstrated that while the historical dimension was an important reason for the travel behaviour of one group studied, they were not able to find any demographic differences distinguishing this group from the non-historians. In common with other market research studies of travel motivation (cf. Goodrich, 1979; Woodside and Sherrell, 1977; Thompson and Cooper, 1979) a lifestyle analysis of the two groups was undertaken with a series of attitude statements. In this particular study it was demonstrated that those interested in travelling for historical as opposed to ahistorical reasons were also more concerned with the educational value of vacations, tended to stay longer in visited areas and were more concerned with achieving family solidarity and happiness during holiday periods.

This kind of study, as opposed to the macro-analysis of destination images, has the advantage of beginning to interrelate traveller characteristics, thus providing a more complete picture of a traveller sub-group. Within the motivational framework outlined earlier, however, this study is also disappointing in some ways. For example, little attention is paid to the long-term goals of the travellers. A more informative account of the "historian-oriented" segment would be provided by setting the current motivated travel behaviour in a perspective which emphasized both past interest in history-related travel and the future value and rewards of this behaviour. Second, the tourists still get little chance to advance their own interpretations of their behaviour. It can be argued from the attributional perspective that having to account for one's behaviour in the terms prescribed by the researchers limits and re-defines the account of the travellers' behaviour. Thirdly, the multi-motive account of behaviour receives some attention but is not clearly expressed. The basic definition of the travel sample into historian and non-historian-related travellers assumes that this is the important motivational split in the total group. Given the finding that historian travellers are more family-oriented this may not be the case and the real differences in the sample could lie between family-oriented and individual-oriented travellers with different love and belongingness needs. These needs may in turn be correlated with historical interests. The point at issue here is that without some guiding motivational framework with which to differentiate travel samples it is difficult to explore and interrelate traveller characteristics in anything but a descriptive manner. Finally, the notion that some travel motivations represent complex, highly self-determined, personal attempts to achieve intangible life satisfactions is not considered within the scope of the study. Indeed, for historian travellers familiarity with the lives of important figures from the past may provide a stimulus for the contemplation of their own achievements and destiny.

It is apparent from the two examples of market research literature advanced here, and indeed the literature which they represent, that a truly psychological motivational approach is poorly developed in this kind of tourist analysis. There are important signs, however, that the present chapter is not pursuing some idiosyncratic psychological hobby-horse as conceptual analyses by Dann (1977) and Crompton (1979) have much in common with the present approach. Principally both these studies suggest that tourist motivation needs to be served by more subtle, more theoretical and more intra-individual approaches.

Dann (1977) argues that the historical and anecdotal tourist motivation literature can be summed up by the concept of escape, but argues that this concept needs refinement for hypothesis-testing. This concept, which has not been considered so far in this chapter, deserves careful scrutiny not only because of its widespread usage, but also because it relates directly to the broader sociological analysis of Cohen and Taylor (1976) who view escape attempts of all sorts as quests for individual survival and identity in the modern world. Dann shares this type of sociological perspective and argues that escape may be usefully understood in terms of the concepts of anomie and ego-enhancement. In relation to anomie he declares:

> The connection between "what makes tourists travel" and the anomic society from which they come thus acts as a hallmark for the current theoretical perspective. It is claimed that a possible push factor for travel lies in the desire to transcend the feeling of isolation obtained in everyday life, where the tourist simply wishes "to get away from it all". (p. 187)

Implicit in this analysis of the anomic society is the view that individuals have strong needs to belong to a caring, closely interconnected, emotionally rewarding community. From the perspective adopted in this chapter, Dann's analysis of anomie is an implicit restatement of Maslow's love and belongingness needs.

Dann also indicates that travelling may provide the individual with a new social position which can be exploited for personal needs of power and recognition. This aspect of the escape motivation is termed ego-enhancement. In the terminology adopted by Maslow ego-enhancement could be aptly described by the concept of self-esteem needs.

In his study of tourists visiting Barbados, and using sets of questions to elicit information relevant to the two concepts of anomie and enhancement, Dann distinguished two tourist types. One set of tourists were described as predominantly anomic types while another separate group of travellers were classified as ego-enhancement-orientated. The anomic tourists were typically from mainland U.S. and Canadian cities, married, with above average socioeconomic status and were sometimes repeat visitors to Barbados. It was argued that these characteristics were consistent with the kinds of complex, isolating stresses associated with modern urban living where competitiveness at work and the demands of the nuclear family at home characterize everyday existence. Ego-enhancement tourists, on the other hand, were frequently of lower socioeconomic status, more likely to be female and first-time visitors to Barbados, and relatively older than the anomic tourists. Dann argued that the demographic characteristics of the self-enhancement group were consistent with low status roles in the tourists' own countries. Accordingly these tourists emphasized the status and the significance of their international holiday, in short the ego-enhancement functions of travelling. As suggested above the two concepts advanced by Dann closely parallel the love and belongingness needs and the self-esteem needs in Maslow's hierarchy. Dann's scheme fails, however, to consider other complex travel needs such as self-actualization, thus limiting the coverage of his motivational framework. Further, it is unclear from the documentation of his interview procedure whether the tourists' own view of their reasons for travelling involved components other than those outlined by the researcher. That is, from an attribution perspective it is unclear whether we have the researcher's gloss on the situation or the tourists' own explanations for their behaviour. Multi-motive control of behaviour is explicitly rejected by Dann as he conceives the ego-enhancement–anomic motives as polar co-ordinates of a single travel motivation continuum. This assertion awaits empirical verification but it would seem highly likely that travellers could be concerned both with enhancing their status and with reducing the stressful residues of modernity. While it is clear that Dann's study has been concerned with *post-hoc* explanations of travel behaviour, it is not clear from this study that an approach to motivation concerned with predicting travel behaviour could use the same concepts.

In summary this sociological analysis reinforces two of the motivational concepts emphasized in Maslow's hierarchy of needs but fails to satisfy many of the criteria for an adequate account of travel motivation as outlined in this chapter. Perhaps most importantly, however, it has emphasized the individual "push" factors associated with travel and has pointed out that:

> by examining "what makes tourists travel", one is looking at a more elementary (and by implication causally prior) need than a specific reason for choice of resort (of secondary causal nature). Consequently, if one is to go beyond the level of description an investigation of "push" factors is indicated. (p. 186)

A second study, equally concerned with emphasizing the intra-individual forces which promote travel behaviour, is that of Crompton (1979). As a preface to a small-scale empirical study, Crompton reviews previous tourist motivation literature and draws several conclusions which are highly consistent with the present emphasis. In addition to the previously mentioned common emphasis on intra-individual motivational concepts, Crompton also argues that "to expect motivation to account for a large variance in tourist behaviour is probably asking too much since there may be other interrelated forces operating" (p. 409). This re-emphasizes the theme discussed earlier when it is argued that one needs to consider how the concept of motivation is being used because there are both predictive and explanatory uses of the concept and these uses involve differing degrees of specificity and forms of measurement. In his own study Crompton not only attempted to use sociopsychological motives to explain the initial impetus to take a vacation but also attempted to use such concepts to analyse the tourists' choice of destination. By analysing the content of a small number of interviews with middle-class Americans from Boston, Massachusetts and College Station, Texas, Crompton identified seven psychological motives for travelling. These motives were described as representing a "hidden agenda" since respondents initially had some difficulty in articulating their personal needs but were readily able to describe destination characteristics. Crompton's list of motives included escape from a perceived mundane environment, exploration and evaluation of self, relaxation, prestige, regression, enhancement of kinship relationships and facilitation of social interaction. The essentially qualitative nature of the study and the size of the interviewed sample ($N = 39$), prevented an analysis of the independence of the seven motives listed. However Crompton explicitly states that he supports a multi-motive view of the determinants of travel behaviour.

One feature of particular interest which emerged from this study concerns the researcher's observation that respondents distinguished between long-term and short-term pressures or disequilibrium states. The interviewees believed that specific holidays at the right time could alleviate the short-term pressures while the longer-term life dissatisfactions were only partly reduced by a planned programme of future vacations. These two types of disequilibrium should be carefully noted by researchers in the area of work–leisure relationships. It may well be the case that current spillover and compensatory theories of leisure are attending to the short-term disequilibrium states while ignoring the longer-term, less tractable kinds of dissatisfactions. This distinction also closely reinforces the emphasis in achievement motivation which draws attention to long-term motivational goals and incentives. Thus, Crompton's analysis of his tourist's opinions about vacation types is highly congruent with one of the features of travel motivation emphasized previously in this discussion.

A final noteworthy feature of Crompton's motivational analysis is the direct challenge to tourist practitioners that they may be emphasizing the wrong perspective in their advertising and marketing strategies. It can be argued that travel consumers are not motivated by the specific qualities of the destination and its attractions but rather by the broad suitability of the destination to fulfil their particular psychological needs. Conceptualizing holiday destinations according to their capacity to fit human needs may produce some strange and novel mental maps of travel destinations. Instead of distance, culture and climate being used to classify destinations, one can envisage clusters of vacation centres which are predominantly self-exploration, or social interaction or indeed sexual arousal and excitement. As Hill (1965) pointed out when exploring the travel motivation market for Ireland:

> The holiday is psychologically a period during which the individual is hoping to take in and store "internal goods" with which he will return enriched, regenerated and recharged to his own environment. From this point of view the environment in which the holiday is taken has to be perceived as rich in that all these imports are available. (p. 30)

In concluding this review of travel motivation several points warrant emphasis. The strategy adopted to review the travel motivation literature has been directed at providing a broad coverage of the historical analysis and selective representative examples of current market research writing and analysis. Within the sampling limitations of this approach it is apparent that a fully adequate account of travel motivation as outlined earlier in this chapter does not yet exist. This is not to suggest that there have not been some useful and insightful studies conducted in this area, but rather highlights the point that additional factors may be usefully considered in future research efforts. In particular it can be argued that models of travel motivation can be developed by building on the theoretical ideas of self-actualization theory with additional insights from achievement motivation and attribution theory. Such a combination of ideas can provide a broad coverage of travel motives, address problems in measurement and the emerging issue of multi-motive causation of behaviour as well as handling long-term motivational perspectives and the question of intrinsic motivation. As evidence to support the value of the proposed perspective on tourist motivation Chapter 6 in this book will provide an analysis of tourist experiences using some of these motivational guidelines. Issues of tourist motivation, like those concerning the role of the tourist, will also be to the fore in the following two chapters concerned with social interaction among tourists and tourist–environment contact.

As a concluding note, while it is still probably true as Lundberg (1972) suggested that we really do not know why tourists travel, it can be suggested that the present chapter has mapped out some of the requirements that must be met by a decent answer to this question. With these guidelines in mind it is to be hoped that some detailed studies of tourist motivation considered from an emic, long-term, multi-motive and non-deterministic perspective for a particular travel group may soon appear in the motivation literature.

References

ALDERSON, F. A. (1971) *The New Grand Tour*. Newton Abbot: David & Charles.
ALLPORT, G. W. (1937) *Personality: A Psychological Interpretation*. New York: Holt.
ANTHONY, I. (1973) *Verulamium*. Hanley: Wood Mitchell.
ARKES, H. R. and GARSKE, J. P. (1977) *Psychological Theories of Motivation*. Monterey, California: Brooks/Cole.
ATKINSON, J. W. and BIRCH, D. (1970) *The Dynamics of Action*. New York: Wiley.
ATKINSON, J. W. and RAYNOR, J. O. (1975) *Motivation and Achievement*. Washington, DC: Winston.
BECK, R. C. (1978) *Motivation: Theories and Principles*. Englewood Cliffs, NJ: Prentice-Hall.
BRUNNER, E. (1945) *Holiday Making and the Holiday Trades*. London: Oxford University Press.
BURKART, A. J. and MEDLIK, S. (1974) *Tourism*. London: Heinemann.
CANADIAN GOVERNMENT TRAVEL BUREAU (1972) *1970 Motivations to Travel and Vacations Trends*. Ottawa: Canadian Government Travel Bureau.
CASSON, L. (1974) *Travel in the Ancient World*. London: Allen & Unwin.
CLAWSON, M. (1963) *Land and Water for Recreation—Opportunities, Problems and Policies*. Resources for the future policy background series. Chicago: Rand McNally.
COFER, C. N. and APPLEY, M. H. (1967) *Motivation: Theory and Research* (fourth printing). New York: Wiley.
COHEN, S. and TAYLOR, L. (1976) *Escape Attempts*. Harmondsworth: Penguin.
COSGROVE, I. and JACKSON, R. (1972) *The Geography of Recreation and Leisure*. London: Hutchinson University Library.
CROMPTON, J. (1979) Motivations for pleasure vacation. *Annals of Tourism Research*, **6**, 408–24.
CSIKSZENTMIHALYI, M. (1979) *Beyond Boredom and Anxiety*. San Francisco: Jossey-Bass.
DANN, G. (1977) Anomie, ego-enhancement and tourism. *Annals of Tourism Research*, **4**, 184–94.
DECHARMS, R. and MUIR, M. S. (1978) Motivation: social approaches. *Annual Review of Psychology*, **29**, 91–113.
DICHTER, E. (1967) "What motivates people to travel?", Address to the Department of Tourism of the Government of India, Kashmir, October.
DULLES, F. R. (1966) A historical view of Americans abroad. *The Annals of the American Academy of Political and Social Science*, **368**, 11–20.
FEATHER, N. (1975) *Values in Education and Society*. New York: Free Press.
FISHBEIN, M. and AJZEN, I. (1974) Attitudes toward objects as predictors of single and multiple behavioural criteria. *Psychological Review*, **81**, 59–74.
GOODRICH, J. N. (1979) Benefit bundle analysis: an empirical study of international travellers. *Journal of Travel Research*, **16** (2), 6–9.

GRANVILLE, A. B. (1841) *The Spas of England.* London: Houghton & Co.

HIBBERT, C. (1969) *The Grand Tour.* London: Weidenfeld & Nicolson.

HILL, J. M. M. (1965) *The Holiday.* London: The Tavistock Institute of Human Relations.

HUXLEY, A. (1925) *Along the Road.* London: Chatto & Windus.

ITTELSON, W. H., PROSHANSKY, H. M., RIVLIN, L. G. and WINKEL, G. H. (1974) *An Introduction to Environmental Psychology.* New York: Holt, Rinehart & Winston.

LUNDBERG, D. E. (1972) *The Tourist Business.* Chicago, Illinois: Institutions/Volume Feeding Management Committee.

NEVILLE, R. (1971) *Playpower.* London: Paladin.

Oxford Magazine (June 1770). Quoted in HIBBERT, C. (1969) *The Grand Tour.* London: Weidenfeld & Nicolson.

PIMLOTT, J. A. R. (1947) *The Englishman's Holiday.* London: Faber & Faber.

PLINY (1966) *Pliny—Selection from the Letters;* ROBINSON, C. E. (ed.). London: George Allen & Unwin.

PUDNEY, J. (1954) *The Thomas Cook Story.* London: Non Fiction Book Club.

ROKEACH, M. (1968) *Beliefs, Attitudes and Values.* San Francisco: Jossey-Bass.

ROWLING, M. (1971) *Everyday Life of Mediaeval Travellers.* London: B. T. Batsford.

SMITH, A. Quoted in HIBBERT, C. (1969) *The Grand Tour.* London: Weidenfeld and Nicolson.

SMITH, V. L. (1978) *Hosts and Guests.* Oxford: Blackwell.

SOLOMON, P. J. and GEORGE, W. R. (1977) The bicentennial traveller: a life-style analysis of the historians segment. *Journal of Travel Research,* **15** (3), 14–17.

SWINGLEHURST, E. (1974) *The Romantic Journey.* London: Pica Editions.

THOMPSON, J. R. and COOPER, P. D. Additional evidence on the limited size of evoked and inept sets of travel destinations. *Journal of Travel Research,* **17** (3), 23–5.

TWAIN, M. (1869) *The Innocents Abroad.* New York: Airmont (reprinted 1967).

WEINER, B. (1974) *Achievement Motivation and Attribution Theory.* Morristown, NJ: General Learning Press.

WILENSKY, H. L. (1960) Work, careers and social integration. *International Social Science Journal,* **12,** 543–60.

WOLFE, R. I. (1967) Recreational travel: the new migration. *Geographical Bulletin,* **2,** 159–67.

WOODSIDE, A. G. and SHERRELL, D. (1977) Traveller evoked, inept and insert sets of vacation destinations. *Journal of Travel Research,* **16** (1), 14–18.

YOUNG, G. (1973) *Tourism, Blessing or Blight?* Harmondsworth: Penguin.

4

Social Contact Between Tourists and Hosts

Introduction

Most research pieces which have been concerned with the social contact between tourists and their hosts have been predominantly interested in the tourists' impact on the host community. This kind of research has attempted to understand tourism's role in influencing the social order through changes in languages, land tenure and employment (Forster, 1964; White, 1974; Esh and Illith, 1975; Kent, 1977; Lanfant, 1980). In addition there has been a concern with the cultural desecration of community life (Nunez, 1963; Eidheim, 1966; Greenwood, 1978; Smith, 1978; Buck, 1978) as well as with such social problems as begging, prostitution and crime (Turner and Ash, 1975; Jud, 1975; Nicholls, 1976; Urbanowicz, 1977, 1978). Not all of the conclusions about tourist impact have been negative. Some positive social consequences of tourism have included new jobs, community modernization and at times the strengthening of cultural traditions (deKadt, 1979; McKean, 1978; Weston, 1979).

However these areas of enquiry will not be the focus of the present review. Instead, this analysis of the social contact between tourists and hosts will be concerned with the social processes which are at work in tourist–host encounters. Subsequently, the effect of these processes will be discussed by looking at the way in which tourists and hosts view one another.

A discussion of the tourist–host social contact process at a social psychological level needs some justification. The aim of such an analysis is to elucidate general processes and forces which account for the perception and behaviour of the people in contact. This aim is achieved by considering the interpersonal forces (e.g. the number of people present, the context of the meeting, the group membership of the participants) and intra-individual forces (the attitudes, motives and social skills of the individuals) operating in the encounter. However such a search for general processes and parameters must be undertaken with caution. In particular there are political and large-scale sociological frameworks which severely limit the generality of any simple social psychological analysis (cf. Matthews, 1977). These limitations are recognized since it is not being claimed here that an analysis of tourist–host encounters will greatly facilitate an understanding of the cultural and ideological ravages of the tourist industry itself. Such considerations fall outside the theoretical scope of a social psychological approach. What is at issue, however, is the set of claims which are advanced in relation to the quality and intimacy of interpersonal relationships fostered in tourist–local encounters. For example is it the case, as some tourism devotees would have it, that travel builds international understanding through an appreciation of the qualities of the individuals of each nation (Waters, 1966)? Or rather, might it not be that modern tourists, particularly those involved in group travel, have such superficial contacts with the local people that they do no more than reinforce their prevailing stereotypes and prejudices? It is these sorts of claims which will be investigated within our social psychological framework.

An analysis of tourist–host contact situations

A general area of social psychological inquiry which is pertinent to tourist–host contact, is that of culture shock (Oberg, 1960). This term refers to the process and the experience of disillusionment which attend those who come in contact with new cultures. It is generally conceived from the point of view of the sojourner, but may also be extended to include the host communities' response to the visitor (Carpenter, 1974). As suggested in Chapter 2 when the concepts of environment and culture shock were discussed, the term "culture shock" may be seen as a generic expression which subsumes numerous types of problems and difficulties induced by shifting from one culture to another. Gullahorn and Gullahorn (1963) and Sewell (1964) have developed a stage approach to culture shock which emphasizes an early phase of excitement followed by a period of disillusionment which in turn gives way to a slow stage of adaptation. If the traveller returns to his own culture a "re-entry crisis", which involves a difficulty in adapting to the home community, may also occur.

As a general introductory model of culture encounters, the concept of culture shock and its stages provides an interesting, often insightful, framework. It is, however, most appropriate as an analysis of long-term contact, such as occurs in migrant or foreign service situations. Tourist–host encounters, as discussed below, have a number of special qualities which change the extent and nature of culture shock.

Sutton (1967), in a relatively early analysis of tourist–host contact, emphasized five important characteristics of such encounters. He argued that the personal relationships involved were transitory, that both parties were oriented to immediate gratification, that the contact involved was asymmetrical in terms of hosts' knowledge on the one hand and the tourists' money and status on the other, that the situation was novel for the visitor and that there was usually an important cultural distance separating the participants.

It is noteworthy that the characteristics which Sutton emphasized are closely related to the social role definition of the tourist outlined in Chapter 2 of this book, where the tourist role was defined as involving transitory contact; status differences; a marked degree of environmental and personal exploitation; and a concern with souvenir-hunting, photography and visiting famous places with little danger to the tourists and with limited understanding of the local people. This close agreement strengthens the view that there are core features of the tourist–host social encounter.

In Sutton's view the tourist–host contacts may achieve positive results if the parties are keyed to tolerance, the visitor enthusiastic, interested and generous and the host competent in providing services. Negative consequences are likely to ensue when the desire for immediate gratification afflicts both the visitor and the host, and when suspicion and mistrust develop from cultural misunderstandings and misplaced attributions about the other group.

While Sutton concluded his original piece by calling for more empirical descriptions and insightful analyses of these contact situations, it was some 10 years before further substantial accounts of tourist–host encounters were developed. One significant analysis of such contact situations has been provided by Taft (1977) who considered in more detail the topic of coping with an unfamiliar culture. Taft's analysis, albeit indirectly, builds on Sutton's concern for the cultural distance which separates the tourist from the host community. He proposed that language differences, economic and political structures, and the sheer size and formality of the contact cultures, all contribute to the gap separating the tourist from the host community.

Taft's analysis also suggested that there are some less obvious factors which affect culture coping. For instance, the abruptness of the cultural change may be important. Here, Taft argued that refugees usually have more problems coping than do migrants, who have planned their change of circumstances. For tourists, abruptness of change may be important if a large number of quite different cultures are being visited in a short time. Such tourists have little chance to adapt to each host culture. Indeed one can postulate, from a learning theory perspective, that there might well be a negative transfer of training in these settings, in that the phrases, number systems and rituals of one culture may actively interfere with the learning of similar contact skills in other cultures. It is not difficult to imagine tourists on a short South American tour who are vainly trying to speak in the language of one country, count in the number system of a second, and pay with the currency of a third. The confusion of the traveller repeatedly exposed to new

Tourist–host encounters; a study in intergroup diversity.

environments may become so great that even simple things become difficult. The feminist novelist Marilyn French cites one such instance:

> I said si for two weeks after I entered France from Italy, and oui for two weeks after I entered Spain from France. And that's an easy enough word to get right. (p. 190)

Taft also suggests that the salience of the cultural differences to each person's functioning will shrink or expand the cultural gap involved. The individual who insists on strict, well-ordered timetables may feel deeply frustrated in cultural communities with scant regard for punctuality. Similarly, limited bathing facilities will also be salient and annoying for those travellers whose self-image is intimately linked to elaborate daily grooming.

A further factor widening the cultural gap between the contact communities is, according to Taft, the comprehensiveness of the new culture. A migrant, without family or fellow-countrymen, might be forced to cope with the cultural demands of the adopted society almost constantly. Tourists, on the other hand, are frequently quite well insulated from the visited society. A number of American hotel chains deliberately promote themselves as comforting and reassuring all-American oases in the threatening deserts of foreignness. The company of fellow-tourists and tourist guides also serves as a buffer insulating many travellers from the difficulties and possibly some delights of the visited culture.

Taft's analysis of the problems of coping with another culture also leads to some suggestions concerning cognitive and behavioural strategies for dealing with these situations (cf. Argyle, 1975). Before considering the application of these coping strategies to the tourist contact situation, it is necessary to explore further the idiosyncratic properties of this type of cultural interaction. For example, it was suggested above that the tourist, unlike many other cultural sojourners, can escape from the visited culture and avoid uncomfortable levels of contact with the host nationality through in-group interaction and the help proffered by tourist guides. It is important to note in this context that tourists interact with only a select sub-sample of the host community, the majority of whom are used to dealing with tourists. In the following discussion of the role of other tourists and tourist guides in shaping tourist–local contact it should be borne in mind that the local people involved are largely those in the tourist industry itself.

There have been a number of analyses of travel groups and tourist guides. Gorman (1979) in his study of a "five countries in seven days" tour of Europe illustrated the camaraderie and sense of shared purpose ("us" against "them") which developed in one such travel group. In his case-study Gorman noted that one crisis incident which resulted in a black, older female tourist being refused admittance to Belgium, acted as a major catalyst for group conversation and subsequently group solidarity. The common threat of foreignness, manifested in the customs bureaucrats, conquered potentially divisive racial, national and age differences among the tour participants. Gorman also observed a number of incipient cliques forming in the travel group. Such cliques, which were based on age, marital status and sophistication, tended to be short-lived and did not become fully separate entities within the tour party. Gorman neatly illustrates the advantages of the whole group retaining a common identity and purpose while travelling when he comments:

> At lunch in Germany the few individuals with a little knowledge of German became indispensable instrumental leaders, buffers between the group and the outside world in negotiating wine and dessert selection. . . . In France . . . we were saved by the French language capabilities of a very shy woman, previously very marginal. . . . Shifting environmental contingencies meant that virtually every group member had a turn at controlling crucial resources and performing indispensable functions. (Gorman (1979) pp. 481–3)

In concluding his analysis of group formation processes, Gorman suggested that the whole group solidarity noted in his case-study may be atypical of the other package-tour situations. This point will be explored in a later chapter of this book where some direct comments from a number of tourists will be considered. For the present· discussion it is critical to appreciate that the tourist–local contact situation is often mediated through, or occurs in the presence of, significant others from one's own culture. It can be appreciated that this social context has important ramifications for intergroup perception through coalition formation, ingroup–outgroup labelling and social comparison processes (cf. Billig, 1976).

While other tourists form an important social context for tourist–local contact, tour guides, couriers and chaperones play an even more direct and prominent role in mediating intergroup cultural exchanges. There are many tourists who travel by themselves (both very affluent and quite impoverished individuals may prefer to travel alone), but most package tours employ a guide or use key members of the local community to introduce the travellers to the visited locations. Smith (1978) has argued that local guides are often marginal figures in their own community and may in fact provide a distorted view of the host culture to the visitor.

In her studies of Eskimo tourism Smith noted that it was the older, socially marginal Eskimos who were most involved in explaining the Eskimo lifestyle to the tourists. Other analyses such as that of Taft (1977) suggest that cultural mediators may be socially marginal in a positive sense, since a number of special qualities are needed for an individual to bridge the gap between diverse communities. Although the evidence as to what constitutes a good cultural mediator is somewhat meagre, ability to learn languages, know one's community, tolerate others and be personally charming are presumably quite important. Accordingly, the best local tourist guides may be quite exceptional and talented members of their culture.

It is also clear that, in countries such as the U.S.S.R., local tourist guides give highly ritualized accounts of their environment. Such guides may openly refuse to answer questions on poverty and social problems, or they may reply to such enquiries with party-line answers such as "We have no prostitution or crime in Moscow" (*Intourist Magazine*, 1980). Clearly, the quality of the information provided by tour guides can vary enormously, and both through the information provided and by personal example the tourist guide may have a considerable impact on the tourists' perception of the host nationality.

The psychological properties of the group situation associated with the guided tour also merit some attention . It is essentially a context in which the tourist acknowledges the competence of the tour guide and abrogates personal responsibility, at least temporarily, of his own freedom of choice and action. Since there is often a strong informational component associated with the tour, there are important resemblances to teacher–student and parent–child roles inherent in the relationship. As Gatto (1977) observed, using the framework of transactional analysis, tourist guides may be seen as parental figures distributing local insights to their dependent children. Such a situation may produce some strange role incongruities as instanced by university professors being lectured in their own area of competence or being chastised for their lateness or rowdy behaviour (cf. Owen, 1968; Gorman, 1979).

Another perspective on the role of the tour guide is contained in the work of Schmidt (1979), who considered the guided tour in structuralist terms. Schmidt argued that guided tours have become popular because they offer tourists ready solutions to the problems of what to see, how to get there and how to deal with the locals on arrival. In addition guided tours can cater to special interest groups, and by controlling tourist numbers can protect popular tourist sites both by preserving privacy for any individuals in the setting and by controlling direct environmental impact. From the point of view of our analysis of the social processes at work in tourist–local encounters, Schmidt suggests that the presence of a guide legitimizes travel as a leisure activity by emphasizing the educational aspects of sightseeing and by removing many of the tourists' interaction difficulties and anxieties. However, a poor tourist guide can ruin the entire travel experience through insensitivity, communication problems or an authoritarian style projected at the wrong time (Lopez, 1980).

Schmidt also argued that the benefits of having a guide depend on the environmental context. She suggested that guided tours are functional in situations which are internally highly structured (e.g. factories, institutions and whole cities) and which maintain some ongoing purpose other than tourism. In such contexts guides inform the tourist and protect the observed situation. Guides are also useful in more traditional tourist destinations (e.g. museums, historical and environmental sites) but principally serve the tourists' interests in such contexts. In other situations, such as those lacking internal structure (e.g. beaches, small parks, small towns, markets, bazaars) it is argued that guides are not functional for the tourists or the site.

This analysis considerably underestimates the importance of social and cultural divisions between tourists and their hosts. For instance Khuri (1968) and Ritter (1975) discussing tourism in the Arab world both observed that individual tourists continually broke rules of courtesy, etiquette and dress requirements in such places as beaches, small towns and in bargaining situations. The need for tourist guides or some form of cross-cultural education would appear to be very strong indeed in just these situations which Schmidt decribed as unimportant as a setting for guided tours.

In summary, the strength of Schmidt's analysis lies in highlighting the advantage of the successful guided tour for the tourist. A good guide, working in the correct context, provides a relatively safe and secure context for the tourist to collect those authentic experiences which fulfill the individual's motivation for travelling.

It is a common view that analyses such as Schmidt's are missing important elements inherent in the tourist debate. Proponents of this view argue that there is a kind of moral imperative to do without a tourist guide and to maximize one's personal contact with the host nationality. The ability to appreciate the visited culture unaided and through direct contact and experiences is supposed to connote a more successful "mature" type of tourist (cf. Kaplan, 1960). But, as MacCannell (1976) has pointed out, such value orientations and comments on tourist types really constitute a part of the phenomenon to be explained rather than analysis in itself. In other words one needs to be aware of the possibility that the so-called new tourist type is a thinly veiled guise to attempt to understand and include the author's own travel behaviour in the schema being outlined. Often, too, such discussions constitute an attempt to shift the debate from the tourist to the traveller role. In the role space described in Chapter 2 of this book this constitutes a semantic attempt to manoeuvre the concept of tourist closer to that of traveller, overseas student and other more intimate culture contact roles. It is the present view that this discussion of "mature" and morally laudable tourist–travellers misses the point. A tourist, defined experientially, does have difficulty with the local people. Honest recognition that this is a cross-cultural contact problem will be more likely to effect a solution than speculative eulogies on "mature" tourists.

One such constructive approach to tourist–local contact learning can be obtained by considering the cognitive and behavioural adaptations possible in contact situations.

Tourist transport; a social situation, involving its own rules and recreational value.

Attempts to improve tourist–host contact difficulties

On a popular level there is so much written concerning how travellers should behave in, think about, and interpret other cultures that one can identify a whole travel literature industry. Most of these guidebooks recommend a form of behavioural compliance or conformity when the tourist is confronted with new cultural norms. This conformity approach has been a common theme in travel guidebooks for centuries and may be traced to the unlikely source of a conversation between two prominent Christian saints of the third century A.D. Reputedly, St Augustine of Hippo was troubled by the Roman's observation of a fast day on Saturday (the Jewish Sabbath) whereas other communities fasted on Sunday (the Christian Sabbath). St Ambrose of Milan suggested, "Quando hic sum, non jejune Sabbate; Quando Romae sum, jejune Sabbate." This may be literally translated as "When I am here, I do not fast on the Sabbath, when I am in Rome, I do", but has become more widely known as "when in Rome do as the Romans do". The practical consequences of this suggestion are that tourists may have to change their clothing style, eating habits, sleeping times and even topics of conversation so as not to offend their hosts. Specific examples offered in modern guidebooks include advice to female tourists such as:

> When visiting Roman Catholic cathedrals and churches wear a dress— or perhaps a light shawl—which covers the upper arms and shoulders, and the head also if the clergy are of the old school. (*The Travel Book*, p. 105)

Travellers to Continental and Asian destinations are warned:

> In small talk with acquaintances made at a social gathering, avoid asking personal questions or volunteering too much information about yourself. In some circles it is considered bad form even to ask what a man's occupation is or to enquire if he is married and has a family. This is not true in India and Pakistan where it is polite to express an interest in family matters. (*The Travel Book*, p. 107)

The following counsel is offered to male tourists in the Middle East:

> Western men accepting hospitality should not expect to be introduced to the female members of their host's household and it is bad manner to inquire after or refer to them. (*The Travel Book*, p. 109)

Conformity to different behavioural styles is not the only kind of advice offered to would-be tourists. There are also attempts to introduce the guidebook readers to new ways of thinking about and interpreting other cultures. For example there is often an attempt to inform the reader that in Asian and Middle-Eastern cultures shopping is not merely a mechanical transaction between sellers and buyers but a forum for social diversion, entertainment and sometimes extreme forms of emotional arousal. This kind of information is very useful, particularly as there have been reports that tourists frequently break the rules of conduct and etiquette in Middle-Eastern shopping transactions (Khuri, 1968; Ritter, 1975). Similarly, emphasis is often placed on how to interpret time and to appreciate the way different cultures use it as a symbolic device. Again, this is undoubtedly useful information, particularly when the face value of some time-related comments has little to do with their intended meaning. For example "Be there at 7" may mean "be there at 5 minutes to 7" in Japan or "Be there at 7.30" in America. Similarly, "let us do it next week" may mean "let's think about it" in Anglo-Saxon cultures and "the arrangement is off or indefinitely postponed" in Latin American communities (Hall, 1955, 1964).

Emphasis on the cognitive components (knowing what the cultural rules are) and the behavioural components (being able to conform externally to the situation) also characterize more thorough-going psychological approaches to culture education such as "culture assimilators" and social skills training. The culture assimilator is a questionnaire-style training programme which takes the form of a written series of hypothetical incidents or encounters in the to-be-visited culture (Fiedler, Mitchell and Triandis, 1971). While this kind of approach has not been used specifically with tourists, it deserves examination because it is the kind of technique which could be adapted for such uses since it attempts to overcome many of the interaction difficulties discussed above. The trainee has to work through the material at his own speed, selecting from a multiple-choice format the appropriate response to each of a variety of cross-cultural episodes. The incidents are taken from the experiences of people previously involved in the cross-cultural contact. The episodes thus selected are supposed to exemplify potential problem areas. As an illustration, consider the following example, which is of the type used in culture assimilators:

> A New Zealand female student travelling through Asia spent three days staying at the family home of a Thai student friend. She found her friend's parents polite and enjoyed conversing with them. She also greatly enjoyed the food and said so to her hosts. Being keen to improve her speaking skills in Thai she visited the kitchen on the second day of her stay and chatted to the servants about the food and living conditions in the country. That night her Thai friend asked her to leave a day earlier than expected on account of a family sickness. That night at dinner it was apparent that no-one was really very sick.

Which of the following is a correct analysis of the situation? The New Zealand student was politely asked to leave early because:

(1) Young females are not expected to participate in conversation with older Thai couples.

(2) It is an imposition for an acquaintance as opposed to a family member to stay more than one night in a Thai home.

(3) Showing excessive enjoyment of food is considered to be vulgar for women.

(4) Conversing with servants on equal terms is considered to be insulting and demeaning to the host family.

Within the format of a culture assimilator the learner chooses one of the four alternatives and is directed to another page for immediate feedback and an explanation of why that choice is correct or incorrect. In the above example choice no. 4 is the most appropriate because crossing status boundaries as described is frowned upon in the Thai culture (cf. Foa and Chemers, 1967). The effectiveness of the assimilator as a means of assisting the integration of peace corps volunteers and similar groups has been evaluated and found to improve peoples' cross-cultural interpersonal relations (Mitchell *et al.*, 1971). To some extent these positive findings must be questioned since many of the studies have very small samples and do not use appropriate control groups. These limitations may well have induced reactivity and sensitization effects. One must also question the heavy reliance on the cognitive understanding of the rules and norms of a culture from a set of written cues.

Neither the dynamic or emotional nor the performative or behavioural aspects of culture coping are examined by the culture assimilator (cf. Taft, 1977). The dynamic aspect of culture encounters may be defined as the interactant's emotional feel for the culture setting. This subtle quality is often overlooked in cross-cultural training programmes and the culture assimilator with its emphasis on understanding cross-cultural rules of conduct must be included in this criticism. The use of verbal as opposed to visual information provides a further barrier in transferring the rules from the testing context to the actual interactions. Nevertheless, the assimilator has been shown to be useful in a limited way and may profit in the future from the use of video to display critical incidents as well as attempts to integrate the performative and dynamic components of culture contact.

While there have not been any real efforts to address the emotional tones and sensitivities needed in cross-cultural encounters, there have been suggestions that performative components, such as those highlighted by social skills training, could be applied to such situations (Argyle, 1975; Taft, 1977; Trower, Bryant and Argyle, 1978). The subtle differences which exist between cultures in non-verbal behaviour provide ready examples illustrating the potential value of such training. Hall (1955) clearly stimulated much of the subsequent work in this area when he observed that tone of voice, ges-

Travelling To Fiji
From Australia

More and more, Fiji is becoming the regular holiday spot for Australians. They like the friendly welcome they get, and being able to speak the same language as usual. Fiji's a nice healthy country too and you don't need any special injections.

There are lots of airlines and ships linking Australia and Fiji so you can travel when it suits you. But once you get to Fiji there is such a variety of things to do.

Wherever you travel there are bound to be a few formalities and a few things you need to know. This little leaflet is designed to reduce your problems to a minimum.

You'll Need A Current Passport

Fiji is a Dominion and is part of the Commonwealth, like Australia. This means, as a Commonwealth citizen, you just need your up-to-date passport when you arrive. The immigration people in Fiji will issue you with a one month Visitor's Permit when you arrive, no need to apply for any visas before you leave Australia.

What Other Formalities Apply To You?

None really. It's as simple as that. But permanent immigration into Fiji is strictly controlled - for one thing there's not much land in a small island nation like Fiji. Further information on this can be had from the Principal Immigration Office in Suva, the capital of Fiji. Although you don't need injections if you live in Australia, you may be coming from an 'endemic fever' area on the way; in that case you would need smallpox or other appropriate innoculation certificates.

Customs Procedures

There are two Customs channels through which you may choose to pass:

GREEN CHANNEL, if you have nothing to declare beyond the duty-free allowances (one bottle of spirits or two bottles of wine or two bottles of beer; 200 cigarettes or half pound of cigars or a half pound of tobacco; your own used personal effects and other goods to a value of $F20). You may pass straight through the GREEN CHANNEL, unless you are selected by a Customs Officer for a "spot" check.

RED CHANNEL, if you have goods to declare.

We Want You To Be Our Guest

When you get to FIJI WE DON'T WANT YOU TO BE JUST A TOURIST. We want you to be our valued guest. We have a multi-racial community and we know you'll be fascinated with their songs and dances, their foods and their cultures. They too will want to talk with you about your way of life.

If you come to visit us in that frame of mind then we're sure you'll find the people of Fiji the friendliest hosts you've ever stayed with.

Dress

Casual, but remember customs in Fiji are more conservative than back home. Scanty clothing should not be worn in towns or villages.

Reef Walking

During your reef walking excursions please do not break live coral off the reefs. It takes 10 years to grow a coral patch the size of a dinner-plate.

Pollution

We in Fiji are pollution conscious. We will love you more if you'll help keep our beautiful beaches and countryside clean and tidy.

Taxis

Always agree on the price before hand. When in doubt, ask to see the published rate sheet.

School Children

Always make sure that the child who offers to carry your bag or take you shopping shouldn't really be at school.

Sun Bathing

Remember you're under a tropical sun. We advise gradual exposure with the use of a suntan lotion at all times.

Tippings

Tipping is not encouraged in Fiji. Only tip if you feel that someone has given you extra good service.

Driving Licences

Visitors in possession of their current domestic licence are eligible to drive in Fiji.

How To Look After Your Money

World currency values change from time to time but usually your Australian dollar will buy more things in Fiji than it will in Australia. This gives you a sort of bonus on your trip. The chief notes used in Fiji are the $5, $2, and $1 bills plus our own 50 cent note. Coins are 1 cent, 2 cent, 5 cent, 10 cent and 20 cent. There are a number of banks in Fiji and they all know how to look after your money for you and make sure you get the best rate of exchange. You can use the services of the Bank of New Zealand, Bank of Australia and New Zealand, First National City Bank, Barclays Bank, Bank of Baroda and Bank of New South Wales.

The banks are open from 10 a.m. to 3 p.m. on weekdays, and until 4 p.m. on Fridays. They are closed on Saturdays and public holidays.

Cultural rules are sometimes explicitly defined for the tourist

tures, and space and time relationships were key components in the "anthropology of manners". While it is apparent that many universally applicable gestures and emotional expressions exist, some small cross-cultural variations may significantly hamper local–tourist contact. For example, an American visiting Sardinia may be considerably embarrassed to find that the O.K. gesture can be interpreted as a symbol of homosexuality (Morris, 1977). If he then visits Japan he may be confused even further since in that culture the same gesture was traditionally used to refer to money (Morsbach, 1973). Even the basic nodding of the head to express agreement and disagreement has subtle variations in the Eastern parts of the Mediterranean (Collett, 1981). Knowledge about such symbolic gesture meanings would certainly be useful to many tourists, as would information on the social use of space. Watson and Graves (1966), following Hall's pioneering work on this topic, found that Americans tended to think Arabs pushy and threatening because of the latter's preference for more direct, closer and more intimate interaction. If the interaction is of sufficient importance to warrant the cost and effort, specialized training procedures may help to overcome these difficulties (Collett, 1971).

One of the interesting findings from such familiarization and rehearsal programmes is that members of the host culture do seem to prefer those people who have had such cross-cultural social skills training. For most tourists, however, it is only the dramatic social breakdowns and gaffes which could motivate any change in their non-verbal behaviour. Perhaps the best model for tourist cross-cultural education is not one of specialized training but rather better-quality, detailed popular information. A strong case for more widespread and adequate information concerning these cross-cultural differences can be made, particularly, as will be demonstrated in the next section, that it is often small incidents of impolite and inappropriate behaviour which heighten tourist–host friction.

The preceding analysis of tourist–local contact has perhaps overemphasized the negative, dysfunctional aspects of such relationships. To some extent an image has been conveyed of a tourist who is debilitated by linguistic, gestural, spatial, time and status differences. To this image may be added stresses relating to orientation problems, luggage organization, safety and health (Harmon, Masuda and Holmes, 1970; Downs and Stea, 1977; Pearce, 1977b). Clearly, these are general comments and will apply in only limited ways to tourists with specific travel destinations. Nor should it be automatically assumed that all of these variables are perceived negatively by all tourists. For some, there is an excitement and pleasure to be found in orienting oneself in a new city, in speaking a new language, meeting new

FIG. 4.3   Some small communities have initiated attempts at visitor education. *Source:* Fiji Visitors' Bureau.

people, and of coping with the demands of luggage, transport and accommodation. The tourist, unlike the migrant, may never have to leave the euphoric stimulating days of cultural newness; a fact recognized by Oberg (1960) and Gullahorn and Gullahorn (1962) who termed the first period of enthusiasm in the culture-adjustment curve "the tourist phase".

Having considered some of the core processes at work in tourist–host encounters, from the limited perspective of interpersonal behaviour as opposed to macrosociological and economic analysis, attention can be focused on the outcomes of several tourist–local contact situations. In particular, the emphasis will be on the way in which tourists and locals perceive one another as illustrations of the material described in this part of the chapter.

Host perceptions of tourists

A critical distinction in this area of enquiry is that between hosts in technologically advanced communities and hosts from relatively unsophisticated nations. This distinction builds on the analysis of tourist–local contact offered by Sutton, who listed asymmetry of contact as a key issue in understanding such encounters. In situations which involve approximate equivalence of economic status between tourists and the local people, the host perceptions of the tourists are rarely extreme or embittered. For example, in 1978 the English Tourist Board sampled Londoners' attitudes to tourists in their city and found a highly favourable set of reactions. Only 8 per cent of Londoners in the survey thought the city should cut down on its numbers of tourists, and only 14 per cent said they suffered personally from tourists in such spheres as overcrowding of transport and shops. Many Londoners expressed the view that they would like more opportunities to get to know tourists and that the large numbers visiting London gave them a sense of pride in their city. The residents of Soho, South Kensington and Greenwich, who have greater contact with tourists, had greater reservations about increasing tourist numbers in the city, but they too reported a sense of satisfaction with the tourist presence, because they were able to use tourist entertainment facilities.

Rothman (1978), using a similar survey methodology, studied resident reactions to domestic tourists in small coastal towns in the United States. The findings closely paralleled those obtained by the English Tourist Board in relation to Londoners' reactions. In the two Atlantic coast towns studied by Rothman tourists were seen as expanding commercial and municipal services and offering the prospect, which was sometimes realized, of long-term friendships with outsiders. Some negative impacts of tourism included litter, traffic congestion, inflation and noise, but many residents reported being able to cope adequately with these disruptive influences.

The theme that in advanced societies direct contact between tourists and hosts can result in important friendships is given a special emphasis in Israel. Cohen (1971) reports that friendships between young Arab males and tourist girls are sociologically important for this traditionally marginal Arab sub-group. Girls from Western and Northern European countries apparently do not share the local Jewish girls' prejudice against Arab males, and are willing to be escorted around the city, talk about their own societies and occasionally offer sexual favours. These contacts considerably enhance the Arab boys' self-esteem and offer, somewhat remotely, a chance for the Arab youths to escape their troubled Israeli existence where their insecure status, lack of education and restricted job opportunities afford little prospect for the future. While Cohen considers such solutions to be largely illusory, he observes that direct contact with the tourist girls is at least alleviating the "system-generated" tension for some Arab youths.

Occasionally there have been reports of positive attitudes towards tourists from small, technologically unsophisticated communities. Boissevain (1979) noted that young people living on the Mediterranean island of Gozo welcomed links and friendships with tourists. The local youths reputedly saw such contacts as a chance to broaden their own views of the world. Moreover the choice of Gozo, as opposed to the larger more industrialized nearby Malta, was viewed as an indication that the island was desirable, a not unimportant factor in enhancing local self-esteem and identity.

Similarly, Packer (1974), who studied the Turkish town of Bodrum, observed that the locals accepted tourists easily. He argued that a fairly homogeneous tourist population and the cultural heritage of the town which had a history of considerable contact with outsiders accounted for the positive attitudes and acceptance. In her wide-ranging studies of tourism and Eskimo communities Smith (1974) noted that in the settlements of Nome, Point Hope and Gambell, tourists were regarded favourably, probably because the tourist–local contact was extremely brief and infrequent. Perhaps too, as Sutton's structural analysis of touring suggested, the tourists were positively perceived because both groups were keyed to tolerance and mutual interest without an opportunity for gross exploitation or mistrust.

Negative perceptions of tourists and resentment of their presence have been noted in a number of situations where the host community is relatively unsophisticated. An example will serve to illustrate the rather frequent pattern of findings in such status differentiated situations.

Pi-Sunyer (1978) traces the development of negative ethnic attitudes in a Catalan host community of North-eastern Spain. He observes that during the summer season the intensity of tourist contact is high with three tourists for every four residents. This may be contrasted with the situation during the late 1950s when few tourists stayed for longer periods and became individuals or at least recognizable and respected "types" within the Catalan community. The degeneration of the ethnic attitudes can be traced to the advent of mass charter tourism in the late 1960s, which resulted in transitory tourist–local contact and less respect for the Catalan way of life. Two decades ago the few Englishmen who visited the village were recognized as having dignity, though inclined to be a little aloof. With mass tourism the corrective individual positive factors which were applied to the view of Englishmen tended to disappear and the balanced early images solidified into a general stereotype such as "boorish and insular". Pi-Sunyer reports that samples of local conversation would suggest that all French people are pushy and bad-mannered, all Germans are stingy and all Italians are untrustworthy. Such negative images tend to legitimize discrimination against tourists in spheres such as prices of goods and the quality of services.

The findings of Pi-Sunyer's study are repeated in a number of locations. Smith (1974) found that the Eskimo communities with the longest, most sustained tourist local contact were also the most negative. According to Smith attitudes towards the visitors have changed from a positive welcome to negative evaluations and resentment due to the loss of privacy. Similarly Francillon (1975) suggests that in Bali the unfriendly attitude of the locals is always near the surface; there is "a grimace behind the smile". Greenwood (1972) has observed a similar ambivalence in Fuenterrabian in Spain, where he claims the Basques perceive the tourists as necessary but find tourism "unpleasant and conflictful".

A slightly more sinister negative reaction to tourists has been observed in the most densely packed tourist regions of Greece, Hawaii and the Caribbean (Bryden, 1973; Packer, 1977; Kent, 1977; Matthews, 1977). In such situations there is a ready acceptance of tourists' dress and behaviour but the true deterioration in local attitudes is reflected in a new readiness to cheat, victimize and even assault the tourists. It appears that a familiar cycle of intergroup hostility lies behind this development of local resentment. As the number of tourists increase the easy-going, rewarding tourist–host contacts diminish. Negative aspects of some tourists are noted and this crystallizes into a stereotype which is then uniformly applied. When the boundaries between ingroup and outgroup solidify, tourists are no longer seen as potentially rewarding individuals but faceless examples of the exploitative outgroup. There are clear parallels here to the processes of ingroup–outgroup favouritism (Wilder, 1978) and the emergence of aggressive behaviour under conditions of de-individuation (Zimbardo, 1969). One conceivable way to prevent this cycle of stereotyping may be a carefully controlled governmental programme monitoring tourist numbers in small communities.

The negative perceptions of tourists bear out the structural elements of the tourist–host encounters emphasized by Sutton (1964), Taft (1977), Bryden (1973) and others. Situations involving asymmetry of frequent, transitory contact, the opportunity for exploitation, and considerable cultural differences between the parties which produces a host of small interaction difficulties, provide the ingredients for considerable tourist–host friction. Naturally, each tourist–host contact situation reviewed above contains some variation from this general overview, but most of the situations considered are characterized by at least two or three of the above factors. This suggests that our understanding of the hosts' perception of tourists is beginning to define some key features which trigger psychological processes of ingroup–outgroup identification, de-individuation, negative affect and hostility. While all of these processes need not be present at once it appears that marked asymmetry of frequent, transitory contact with the opportunity for exploitation and interaction difficulties due to large cultural differences are the important elements shaping a negative host reaction to tourists.

Tourists' perceptions of the local people

Tourists' reactions to their hosts have not been studied as frequently as the hosts' reactions to the tourists. Considerable claims are often advanced for the ennobling effects of travel—it is "fatal to prejudice, bigotry and narrow-mindedness" claimed Mark Twain—but the empirical evidence to support such enthusiastic suggestions is at best equivocal.

Two kinds of empirical evidence are relevant here. There are large-scale national surveys of tourists' post-travel attitudes and smaller psychological studies of particular instances of travel as a form of ethnic contact. Both these types of evidence will be discussed. It is necessary to preface such discussion with the reminder that there is considerable variation in the types of traveller roles examined in the following studies. Several accounts may be seen to be more properly concerned with the international student role rather than the tourist role (cf. Chapter 2). Nevertheless such studies are included here because of the paucity both of direct tourist studies and of sufficient parallels between the student studies and tourist studies to permit comparison and analogies.

The large-scale surveys

In a series of surveys conducted by the British Tourist Authority, overseas visitors were asked about their attitudes to holidays in Britain. The responses differed according to the tourists' country of origin. Thus, Americans commented on the polite and helpful nature of the British people and greatly praised the country's cultural association and scenery (BTA, 1972a). Canadian tourists to Britain were impressed by the country's historical and cultural associations, while other favourable comments were directed towards the courtesy of the people and the country's scenery and landscape (BTA, 1972b). Studies of European tourists in Britain indicated a wide diversity of motivations for travelling, but many of the wealthier Dutch, German and French travellers praised the interesting cities and museums while remaining rather neutral towards the British people and their way of life (BTA, 1972c). Not all such surveys indicate clear images of Britain after holidaying there. Twenty-five per cent of Brazilian visitors, including Britain on their trips around Europe, were unable to name anything particularly attractive about their visit (BTA, 1973).

Similar research was conducted by Shipka (1978) with regard to America as a holiday destination for Europeans. Some improvements in how Americans were perceived included the perception that Americans were friendlier than imagined, the country safer than its image connoted, and that prices were not exorbitant. This large-scale survey work provides some general evidence that many travellers form clear images of the countries they visit. However, to understand precisely how these images alter, a more systematic measurement and comparison of pre- and post-travel attitudes is required.

Small-scale social psychological studies of tourist attitude change

Studies of stereotyping and ethnic contact in social psychology have general implications for a model of tourist attitude change following intercultural experiences. Since the bulk of the contact research is concerned with overseas students and their images of the visited nationalities, only selected studies will be reviewed here in detail.

An early study of the effects on tourists of intercultural contact is provided by Smith (1955, 1957). Young Americans who spent a summer touring Europe were sent a mail questionnaire, both before and after their travels. The questionnaire contained ethnocentrism, fascism and conservatism scales. A stay-at-home group of similar students served as controls. Behavioural indices (such as gifts and correspondence to Europe) were also used to assess the effect of the trip on the students' attitudes. Smith reported few attitudinal changes on the scales used, and concluded that deeply rooted attitudes were not affected by the travel experience. For the few subjects who did change their attitudes Smith argued, following interviews with the travellers, that the change took place more for attitudes held due to peer conformity pressures than due to some functional personality need of the individual. The brief European excursion had fostered some contacts with the hosts, since most travellers exchanged correspondence and gifts. A follow-up study revealed that in a few cases these relationships persisted for up to 4 years, but only where intense personal relationships had been established (Smith, 1957). It can also be claimed from this research that travel may operate as a "sleeper" effect, since 4½ years later many of Smith's subjects were less ethnocentric and authoritarian. The difficulty of such an

Tourist–host encounters involving eating, drinking and shopping may contain more problems than is apparent from the smiles depicted in tourist brochures.

interpretation lies in distinguishing the travel effects from the larger social and cultural changes of opinion taking place in the American community in the same time-period. In addition, many of these students may have had additional travel experiences and cross-cultural contacts in the intervening years. These kinds of methodology problems have been underestimated in evaluating the effects of cross-cultural experience (cf. Bochner, Lin and McLeod, 1979).

Further ethnic contact research attitude change among travellers has been conducted by Triandis and colleagues (Triandis *et al.*, 1966; Triandis and Vassiliou, 1967; Triandis, 1972). As well as providing some useful conceptual distinctions, this programme of work, and the study of Triandis and Vassiliou in particular, highlights some of the problems of research in this field. Triandis and Vassiliou studied three groups of Americans who had varying contact with Greeks, and three Greek groups with differing contact experiences with Americans. These groups were principally Greek students and American military personnel, and the intercultural experiences involved travelling and meeting the other nationality in their own country. The researchers distinguished heterostereotypes (images of another nationality) from autostereotypes (images of one's own nationality). They predicted, according to an unequal status assessment of the contact situation, that Americans would devalue Greeks but not themselves, while Greeks would see Americans more positively but the Greek autostereotype would suffer. This status interpretation held for the American sample but not for the Greek students in America, who managed to evaluate Americans more positively, without denigrating themselves.

The problems raised by this study are of a general and pervasive nature in studying travellers' attitudes and responses to intercultural contact. Firstly, it is usually difficult to obtain strictly comparable groups in this kind of work. The findings may be equally well explained by the nature of the samples of students and servicemen chosen. Secondly, the effects of sensitizing the travellers to the researchers' hypotheses frequently appears in such studies. A stay-at-home control group of similar educational and socioeconomic status is a basic prerequisite for evaluating travel effects (cf. Campbell and Stanley, 1966). Another contribution of the Triandis and Vassiliou paper is to show how important the tourists motives are in trying to understand intercultural contact, enabling the researcher to clarify the purpose of the contact and hence its meaning for the participants.

Another study more directly concerned with assessing tourists' attitudes to the visited nationality was conducted amongst British tourists visiting either Greece or Morocco (Pearce, 1977, 1980). This study will be discussed in some detail as it is specifically aimed at assessing tourists' post-travel attitude changes. The tourists studied were young members of cheap package tours on 2–3-week tours of either country. A set of questions concerning their travel motivations revealed that they were predominantly interested in relaxing, drinking and having a good time with fellow-travellers in novel, sunny settings, and that they were not particularly motivated by a desire to meet the local inhabitants or study their culture. A group of control subjects who were interested in travel but could not join these particular groups for time scheduling reasons were used to assess test sensitization and measurement effects in the questionnaire. Four aspects of the tourists' attitudes to the local people were tested by comparing their responses 1 week before the overseas holidays, and 1 week after the tourists had returned to Britain. The four central questions were as follows:

(1) Would the travellers change their overall evaluation of the visited nationality?
(2) What beliefs (if any) about the visited nationality would change due to the travel experience?
(3) Would the tourists have more confidence in their beliefs after their holidays?
(4) Would the tourists begin to differentiate the visited community by noticing social class, ethnic and racial groups rather than responding to the community as a whole?

The results for the tourists to Greece and the tourists to Morocco were somewhat different but a number of changes were recorded for both tourist groups, while the non-travelling control group showed no significant changes in any of the four areas under review. This lack of change in the control group strengthens the view that the effects obtained are due to travelling as opposed to questionnaire sensitization. To appreciate the results obtained in the study of travellers to Greece and Morocco a preliminary methodological issue must be discussed.

Many studies of attitude change and intercultural contact use a list of beliefs or scales describing the hosts, and evaluate changes along these scales. This approach is adequate provided the appropriate scales have been chosen. In order to ensure that all relevant dimensions were employed in the second part of the study, a multi-dimensional scaling analysis of stereotyped descriptions of Moroccans and Greeks was initially undertaken. This provided a two-dimensional picture of 50 stereotyped adjectives and 20 such terms were then chosen to sample the full range of meaning inherent in the semantic space describing these national groups. For the tourists to Greece the results showed that the travellers saw the Greeks as less suave, more religious and less affluent than they did prior to their holidays. An unexpected effect was obtained in the belief statements, where the British tourists also changed one of their beliefs about their fellow-countrymen during the same period. The returning tourists saw the British people as more affluent than they did before the holiday experience. The effect of a direct comparison with the visited country may well have been responsible for this change. This kind of change of belief by comparison with a new external standard of reference has parallels in the psychological principle of perceptual adaptation level (Helson, 1948).

The pattern of findings for the tourists to Morocco had some rather different features. The Moroccans were evaluated less favourably on the global score of liking following the tourists' holidays. The beliefs which changed between the two testing periods were that the Moroccans were poorer than imagined, more conservative, more talkative, more musical, more tense, and exhibited more mercenary and greedy characteristics than envisaged. The tourists to Morocco also changed some of their perceptions of the British after travelling. Their fellow-countrymen were now seen as less tense and more affluent than prior to the travel experience. Again the notions of a new standard of reference and social comparison might be suggested as the bases for this change. The finding that tourists can make some small-scale re-evaluations of their own countrymen after travelling abroad parallels findings for students living abroad, who also alter their perceptions of home (Herman and Schild, 1960; Riegel, 1953; Useem and Useem, 1967).

Another aspect of the Pearce study related tourists' changes in belief about the local people to the confidence with which these beliefs were initially held. It was demonstrated, for the tourists to Greece and to Morocco, that the travellers' initial confidence in their beliefs influenced the changes which occurred, since the beliefs which were most likely to change were those which were held less confidently. Overall, though, the tourists' confidence in their views about the Greeks and Moroccans increased. This pro-

TABLE 4.1   *Travellers' changes in beliefs about their hosts and their own nationality* (after Pearce, 1977)

TRAVELLERS TO GREECE Post-travel changes in beliefs about:		TRAVELLERS TO MOROCCO Post-travel changes in beliefs about:	
The Greeks	Own nationality	The Moroccans	Own nationality
Suave* (−)†		Tense (+)	Tense (−)
Religious (−)		Greedy (+)	
Poor (+)	Poor (−)	Mercenary (+)	
Rich (−)		Poor (+)	Poor (−)
		Rich (−)	
		Conservative (+)	
		Talkative (+)	
		Musical (+)	

* All items reported here were shown to be significantly different in the post-travel testing from the pre-travel testing using *t* test for related samples at the 0·01 level of significance.

† The sign (−) refers to a perceived decrease in the characteristic, and the sign (+) refers to a perceived increase in the post-travel belief statement.

vides some empirical support for the familiar phenomenon of the returning tourist brashly asserting that he or she now knows all about the locals and the country in question (cf. Lundberg, 1972).

The notion was not supported that the tourist is a kind of amateur ethnographer collecting information and forming differentiated hypotheses, albeit somewhat unsubtle ones, about the local people (cf. MacCannell, 1976). The two groups of tourists did not perceive significantly more cultural sub-groupings (such as Berbers and French in Morocco, or Turks and Cypriots in Greece) following their travel experiences. However, this does not directly contradict MacCannell's assertion that the analogy of tourist as an amateur scientist (cf. Kelly, 1955) is appropriate for some tourists, since it must be recalled that the motivations of the British travellers under review were not oriented in the direction of social contact with the locals.

Two other studies of tourists' post-travel attitudes have also recently appeared in the psychological literature. Steinkalk and Taft (1979) have assessed the effect of a planned holiday in Israel for Australian tertiary students, while Cort and King (1979) investigated the attitudes and difficulties experienced by university-sponsored American tourists in East Africa. In the Steinkalk and Taft study the touring group and a control group completed questionnaires before and after the tour, as well as filling in semantic differential scales on concepts relevant to Israel and Australia. The biases of the tour group, which had rated Israel kibbutz life more positively than the control group in the pre-tour assessment, were reinforced by the travel experience as in their post-travel assessments they were even more favourable towards kibbutz life. Similarly the experience of the travel group tended to confirm pre-existing opinions about the relationship between Israeli Jews and Arabs. As in the Pearce study, there was a tendency for a number of the tour participants (35 per cent) to comment that their travel had resulted in greater insight into their own culture.

There was also some evidence that the tour participants had incorporated some Israeli behaviour (chiefly a few words and new foods) into their own Australian style of living). In general the travellers' attitudes towards Israel tended to move in a favourable direction after the tour, but it must be stressed that this group of tourists shared to some extent the role characteristics of international students. Each tour member was involved in lectures and seminars in Israel, they spent evenings with Israeli families and for most of the trip were accompanied by Israeli guides, drivers and tour organizers. Within the traveller role space presented in Chapter 2 it is apparent that the positive attitude changes reported here must be considered to apply to roles which are somewhere in between the tourist role as strictly defined and the international student role.

Cort and King (1979) analysed the attitudes and cross-cultural contact processes experienced by a somewhat more typical group of tourists in East

Africa. Again, the tourists had tertiary education and were involved in a study tour, but had more free time and fewer scheduled activities involving the local people than did the travellers in Steinkalk and Taft's study. The researchers were particularly interested in culture shock symptoms in the tourists and endeavoured to assess cultural withdrawal and hostility towards Africans through tour leaders' ratings and questionnaires as well as a number of personality measures. The principal finding was that the intolerance of ambiguity personality measure was correlated positively with the measures of culture shock, presumably because such a personality disposition magnified the stressful aspects of the African setting. Interestingly, despite the considerable cultural gap between East Africa and the United States, many of the tourists did not develop the predicted high levels of culture shock and the hostility level towards the African people was frequently very low. In fact some of the testing questions had to be omitted from Cort and King's analysis because "too few people experienced culture shock". It would appear, then, that even when researchers deliberately seek tourists' negative responses towards the host community, and despite the self-fulfilling prophecies and reactivity effects which such an approach generates, tourist response to the local people is often quite favourable.

The above three studies have been considered in some detail because they are typical of a small corpus of work which has attempted to evaluate empirically the much-vaunted claims and counterclaims concerning positive and negative attitude effects due to travel. Admittedly, these studies have their inadequacies. It is only possible to study particular, specific tour groups, all of which relate slightly differently to the core tourist role described in Chapter 2. There has been little attention in these studies to the travellers' motivation, which could significantly affect their response to the local people. Most of the studies have small sample sizes, and despite the use of control groups there are undoubtedly some reactivity and test-sensitization effects involved (cf. Bochner, Lin and McLeod, 1979).

Further studies involving different travel arrangements and samples will undoubtedly be able to build on the few published findings. For the present, however, the prevailing view inherent in the research would appear to suggest that tourists do develop, albeit marginally, more positive attitudes to their hosts as a consequence of their travelling. This trend may well be consistent with another explanation of the effects of travelling on attitudes, which holds that holiday experiences tend to confirm pre-existing attitudes. When pre-travel attitudes are favourable, marginally more positive evaluations are usually obtained. However, if the pre-travel attitudes are slightly negative, as in the case-study of British attitudes to Moroccans, the confirmation and strengthening of pre-travel attitudes results in more unfavourable assessments (cf. Pearce, 1980). This line of enquiry offers scope for further analysis with a range of tourist destinations and a variety of pre-travel evaluations.

The findings discussed in this section of the chapter do not relate neatly to the structural analysis of tourist contact situations offered earlier. First, as argued above it is difficult to provide a general conclusion about tourists' perceptions of their hosts. This difficulty is in part due to the small number of studies but is also a product of the diversity of tourist–local contact. Unlike the studies dealing with the hosts' perceptions of tourists where in all cases there is an identifiable common target, the research concerned with tourists' views of their hosts must expect great variability in the tourists' responses because of the diversity of the hosts themselves.

More simply, there are just too few studies on too few hosts to permit generalization. In addition, the studies which exist tend to report broad attitudinal outcomes of the travel experience. Little has been done to provide information on tourists' behavioural responses to the host community. One can also ask whether there is an increased cognitive understanding of the host culture since this too has not been documented, although there is evidence that factual information about the visited community is obtained (Downs and Stea, 1977).

Nevertheless, it is anticipated that the structural features of tourist–local contact situations reviewed earlier, and which were shown to be of considerable use in understanding locals' perceptions of tourists, may also provide a valuable framework for tourists' responses to their hosts. Some possible developments in the assessment of tourists' attitudes to the local people have already been foreshadowed. It would be particularly interesting and useful to see such attitudinal studies supplemented by new behavioural and cognitive approaches.

References

ARGYLE, M. (1975) *Bodily Communication*. London: Methuen.

BILLIG, M. (1976) *Social Psychology and Intergroup Relations*. London: Academic Press.

BOCHNER, S., LIN, A. and McLEOD, M. (1979) Cross-cultural contact and the development of an international perspective. *Journal of Social Psychology*, **107**, 29–41.

BOISSEVAIN, J. (1979) The impact of tourism on a dependent island: Gozo, Malta. *Annals of Tourism Research*, **6**, 76–90.

BRITISH TOURIST AUTHORITY (1972a) The Chicago workshop: The United States travel market. *Research Newsletter*, **7** (Winter).

BRITISH TOURIST AUTHORITY (1972b) The Toronto workshop: The Canadian travel market. *Research Newsletter*, **7** (Winter).

BRITISH TOURIST AUTHORITY (1972c) Attitudes to travel among affluent adult holidaymakers in Holland, Germany and France—1972. *Research Newsletter*, **6** (Autumn).

BRITISH TOURIST AUTHORITY (1973) Travellers to the U.K. from Brazil and the Argentine—1972. *Research Newsletter*, **10** (Autumn).

BRYDEN, J. (1973) *Tourism and development: Case study of Commonwealth Caribbean*. Cambridge: Cambridge University Press.

BUCK, R. (1978) Boundary maintenance revisited: tourist experience in an old order Amish community. *Rural Sociology*, **43** (2), 221–34.

CAMPBELL, D. and STANLEY, J. (1966) *Experimental and Quasi-experimental Designs for Research*. Chicago: Rand McNally.

CARPENTER, E. S. (1974) *Oh, what a Blow that Phantom Gave Me!* New York: Holt, Rinehart & Winston.

COHEN, E. (1971) Arab boys and tourist girls in a mixed Jewish–Arab community. *International Journal of Comparative Sociology*, **12**, 217–33.

COLLETT, P. (1971) Training Englishmen in the non-verbal behaviour of Arabs. *International Journal of Psychology*, **6**, 209–15.

COLLETT, P. (1981) The function of gestures in cross-cultural communication. In BOCHNER, S. (ed.) *Studies in Cross-Cultural Interaction*. Oxford: Pergamon.

CORT, D. and KING, M. (1979) Şome correlates of culture shock among American tourists in Africa. *International Journal of Intercultural Behaviour*, **3** (2), 211–26.

DEKADT, E. (ed.) *Tourism: Passport to Development? Perspectives on the Social and Cultural Effects in Developing Countries*. New York: Oxford University Press.

DOWNS, R. and STEA, D. (1977) *Maps in Minds*. New York: Harper & Row.

EIDHEIM, H. (1966) Lappish guest relationships under conditions of cultural change. *American Anthropologist*, **68**, 426–37.

ENGLISH TOURIST BOARD (1978) Study of Londoners' attitudes to tourists. *Journal of Tourist Research*, **17**, 19.

ESH, T. and ILLITH, R. (1975) Tourism in developing countries: trick or treat? A report from the Gambia. Scandinavian Institute of African Studies, Sweden. *Research Report*, no. 31.

FIEDLER, F. E., MITCHELL, T. R. and TRIANDIS, H. C. (1971) The culture assimilator: an approach to cross-cultural training. *Journal of Applied Psychology*, **55**, 95–102.

FOA, V. G. and CHEMERS, M. M. (1967) The significance of role behaviour differentiation for cross-cultural interaction training. *International Journal of Psychology*, **2** (1), 45–57.

FORSTER, J. (1964) The sociological consequences of tourism. *International Journal of Comparative Sociology*, **5**, 217–27.

FRANCILLON, G. (1975) *Bali: Tourism, Culture, Environment*. Report No. SHC-75/WS/17. Bali, Indonesia and Paris: Universitas Udayana and UNESCO.

FRENCH, M. (1978) *The Women's Room*. Glasgow: Sphere.

GATTO, J. (1977) An overview of TA (Transactional Analysis). *Eighth Annual Conference Proceedings. The Travel Research Association*, pp. 151–8.

GORMAN, B. (1979) Seven days, five countries. *Urban Life*, **7** (4), 469–91.

GREENWOOD, D. J. (1972) Tourism as an agent of change: a Spanish Basque case. *Ethnology*, **9**, 80–90.

GREENWOOD, D. J. (1978) Culture by the pound: an anthropological perspective on tourism as cultural commoditization. In SMITH, V. L. (ed.) *Hosts and Guests*. Oxford: Blackwell.

GULLAHORN, J. E. and GULLAHORN, J. T. (1963) An extension of the U-curve hypothesis. *Journal of Social Issues*, **19**, 33–47.

HALL, E. T. (1955) The anthropology of manners. *Scientific American*, **192** (4), 84–8.

HALL, E. T. (1964). Adumbration as a feature of interculturation communication. *American Anthropologist*, **6** (2), 154–63.

HARMON, D. K., MASUDA, M. and HOLMES, T. H. (1970) The social readjustment rating scale: a cross cultural study of Western Europeans and Americans. *Journal of Psychosomatic Research*, **14**, 391–400.

HELSON, H. (1948) Adaptation level as a basis for a quantitative theory of frames of reference. *Psychological Review*, **55**, 297–313.

HERMAN, S. and SCHILD, E. (1960) Contexts for the study of cross-cultural education. *Journal of Social Psychology*, **52**, 231–50.

Intourist Magazine. "Moscow 1980: the people's games". January edition. Moscow: U.S.S.R.

JUD, D. G. (1975) Tourism and crime in Mexico. *Social Science Quarterly*, **56** (2), 324–36.

KAPLAN, M. (1960) *Leisure in America: A Social Inquiry*. New York: Wiley.

KELLY, G. A. (1955) *The Psychology of Personal Constructs*. New York: Norton.

KENT, N. (1977) A new kind of sugar. In FINNEY, B. R. and WATSON, K. A. (eds) *A New Kind of Sugar: Tourism in the Pacific*. Honolulu, Hawaii: The East–West Center.

KHURI, F. I. (1968) The etiquette of bargaining in the Middle East. *American Anthropologist*, **70**, 698–706.

LANFANT, M. (1980) Introduction: tourism in the process of internationalization. *International Social Science Journal*, **32** (1), 14–43.

LOPEZ, E. M. (1980) The effects of leadership style on satisfaction-levels of tour quality. *Journal of Travel Research*, **18** (4), 20–3.

LUNDBERG, D. E. (1972) *The Tourist Business*. Chicago: Institutions Volume Feeding Management Committee.

MACCANNELL, D. (1976) *The Tourist*. New York: Schocken.

MATTHEWS, H. G. (1977) Radicals and third world tourism: a Caribbean focus. *Annals of Tourism Research*, **5**, 20–9.

MCKEAN, P. F. (1978) Towards a theoretical analysis of tourism: economic dualism and cultural involution in Bali. In SMITH, V. (ed.) *Hosts and Guests*. Oxford: Blackwell.

MITCHELL, T. R., DOSSETT, D., FIEDLER, F. E. and TRIANDIS, H. (1971) *Cultural Training: Validation Evidence for the Culture Assimilation*. University of Washington and University of Illinois Technical Report, pp. 71–128.

MORRIS, D. (1977) *Manwatching*. London: Jonathan Cape.

MORSBACH, H. (1973) Aspects of nonverbal communication in Japan. *Journal of Nervous and Mental Disease*, **157**, 262–77.

NICHOLLS, L. L. (1976) Crime detection and law stabilization in tourist-recreation regions: a conference report. *Journal of Travel Research*, **15**, 18–20.

NUNEZ, T. A. (1963) Tourism, tradition and acculturation: weekendismo in a Mexican village. *Ethnology*, **2** (3), 347–52.

OBERG, K. (1960) Cultural shock: adjustment to new cultural environments. *Practical Anthropology*, **7**, 177–82.

OWEN, C. (1968) *Britons Abroad*. London: Routledge & Kegan Paul.

PACKER, L. V. (1974) Tourism in the Small Community: A Cross-cultural Analysis of Developmental Change. Unpublished PhD dissertation, University of Oregon.

PEARCE, P. L. (1977a) The Social and Environmental Perceptions of Overseas Tourists. Unpublished DPhil. dissertation, University of Oxford.

PEARCE, P. L. (1977b) Mental souvenirs: a study of tourists and their city maps. *Australian Journal of Psychology*, **29**, 203–10.

PEARCE, P. L. (1980) A favorability–satisfaction model of tourists' evaluations. *Journal of Travel Research*, **14** (1), 13–17.

PI-SUNYER, O. (1978) Through native eyes: tourists and tourism in a Catalan maritime community. In SMITH, V. (ed.) *Hosts and Guests*. Oxford: Blackwell.

RIEGEL, O. W. (1953) Residual effects of exchange of persons. *Public Opinion Quarterly*, **17**, 319–27.

RITTER, W. (1975) Recreation and tourism in Islamic countries. *Ekistics*, **236**, 56–9.

SCHMIDT, C. J. (1979) The guided tour. *Urban Life*, **7** (4), 441–67.

SHIPKA, B. (1978) 1978 International travel outlook. *Proceedings 1978 Travel Outlook Forum*. Washington: United States Travel Data Center, pp. 133–57.

SMITH, H. P. (1955) Do intercultural experiences affect attitudes? *Journal of Abnormal and Social Psychology*, **51**, 469–77.

SMITH, H. P. (1957) The effects of intercultural experience: a follow-up investigation. *Journal of Abnormal and Social Psychology*, **54**, 266–9.

SMITH, V. L. (1974) Eskimo perceptions of tourists in four Alaskan communities. Paper read at the Annual Meeting of the American Anthropological Association, 24 November 1974.

SMITH, V. L. (1978) Eskimo tourism: micro-models and marginal men. In SMITH, V. L. (ed.) *Hosts and Guests*. Oxford: Blackwell.

STEINKALK, E. and TAFT, R. (1979) The effect of a planned intercultural experience on the attitudes and behaviour of the participants. *International Journal of Intercultural Relations*, **3** (2), 187–98.

SUTTON, W. A. (1967) Travel and understanding: notes on the social structure of touring. *International Journal of Comparative Sociology*, **8**, 217–23.

TAFT, R. (1977) Coping with unfamiliar cultures. In WARREN, N. (ed.) *Studies in Cross-cultural Psychology*, vol. 1. London: Academic Press.

The Travel Book (1978) Melbourne: Chartwell Press.

TRIANDIS, H. C. (1972) *The Analysis of Subjective Culture*. New York: Wiley.

TRIANDIS, H. C. and VASSILIOU, V. (1967) Frequency of contact and stereotyping. *Journal of Personality and Social Psychology*, 7, 316–28.

TROWER, P., BRYANT, B. and ARGYLE, M. (1978) *Social Skills and Mental Health*. London: Methuen.

TURNER, L. and ASH, J. (1975) *The Golden Hordes*. London: Constable.

URBANOWICZ, C. (1977) Integrating tourism with other industries in Tonga. In FARRELL, B. (ed.) *The Social and Economic Impact of Tourism on Pacific Communities*. Santa Cruz: Center for South Pacific Studies, University of California.

URBANOWICZ, C. (1978) Tourism in Tonga: troubled times. In SMITH, V. (ed.) *Hosts and Guests*. Oxford: Blackwell.

USEEM, J. and USEEM, R. (1967) The interfaces of a binational third culture; a study of the American community in India. *Journal of Social Issues*, 23, 130–43.

WATERS, S. R. (1966) The American tourist. *Annals of the American Academy of Political and Social Science*, 368, 109–18.

WATSON, O. M. and GRAVES, T. D. (1966) Quantitative research in proxemic behaviour. *American Anthropologist*, 68, 971–85.

WESTON, C. R. (1979) *The Social Costs and Benefits of Foreign Tourism in Australia*. Report to the Bureau of Industry Economics, Canberra, Australia.

WHITE, P. E. (1974) *The social impact of tourism on host communities: A study of language change in Switzerland*. School of Geography, University of Oxford Research Paper No. 9.

WILDER, D. (1978) Reduction of intergroup discrimination through individuation of the out-group. *Journal of Personality and Social Psychology*, 36, 1361–74.

ZIMBARDO, P. (1969) The human choices: individuation, reason and order versus de-individuation, impulse and chaos. In ARNOLD, W. J. and LEVINE, D. (eds) *Nebraska Symposium on Motivation*, vol. 1. Lincoln: University of Nebraska Press.

5

Tourists and the Environment

Introduction

It is a consistent motif of this book that a concerted emphasis on the tourists' social behaviour and psychological appraisal of the tourist situation will advance the study of tourism. The emphasis in this chapter, which is concerned with the environmental settings of tourist behaviour, is consistent with this guiding motif. Throughout, this appraisal of tourists and the environment will seek to document the tourists' phenomenological experience of holiday destinations.

There are, of course, several other approaches to the general area of tourist–environment concern. For example, the environmental effects of tourism and tourists command considerable attention (Bosselman, 1979; Cohen, 1978). Within this framework a number of comprehensive sources have documented the predominantly deleterious effects of the tourist industry on the ecological, cultural and geographical features of the environment (Cohen, 1978; Farrell, 1977; Turner and Ash, 1975; Pearce, 1981). Examples of the tourist industry polluting pristine environments include irreparable foreshore and sand-dune damage to some of the world's greatest beaches in Honolulu (Potter, 1972) due to high-rise buildings and the ensuing ecological changes to the foreshore environment.

The physical press of large numbers of human beings has its own negative consequences in specially sensitive settings. For example, the world-famous cave paintings at Lascaux have deteriorated alarmingly due to the visiting tourists breathing near the murals. As Morris (1979) noted: "The human moisture and gases were rapidly disintegrating the precious frescoes and in a space of twenty years of exposure to modern humanity, the great works of art that had been perfectly preserved for twenty thousand years previously had been obliterated."

As Nicholson (1972) has pointed out, many people fail to grasp the number of ecological factors which are very seriously affected by tourism. The list includes such effects as noise, litter, souveniring, fires, erosion,

97

roads and developmental pressures such as facility construction, resource degradation and a host of other environmental offshoots. Sometimes, however, tourism and tourists receive the blame when there are other developmental or habitat pressures influencing the ecosystem. Thus it is a little hard to believe Nicholson's report that the chamois in Yugoslavia were leaping to their death in mass suicide as a consequence of tourists' bad attempts at yodelling!

A balanced appraisal of tourist impact on the environment must also stress the beneficial effects of tourist interest and money in conserving, restoring and rescuing tourist sites. The historic houses of Britain are obvious examples of tourism's contribution to environmental preservation through cash from the visitors, but in addition there is a wide net of projects and developments which are more ecologically sensitive and aesthetically pleasing because they are performed with a view to attracting tourists (Cohen, 1978). In the Lucknow region of India, for example, electricity-generating authorities have turned engineering necessities such as dams and power stations into beautified public and tourist parks and recreation areas (Singh, 1979).

These environmental impacts, both of the tourist industry and individual tourists, will not be the focus of this chapter. Instead, four themes of person–environment interaction which feature in social and environmental psychology research will be pursued. It is proposed that analysis of tourist behaviour, with the theoretical guidelines of these areas of conern, will prove to be a profitable way of understanding tourist–environment relationships. Such an analysis may then be employed to address the issue of tourist–environment impact in a more systematic and perhaps less gloomy manner than that which characterizes present writing in this area. The four areas of concern will be the conceptualization of tourist environments, attitude changes to tourist environments, environmental education and interpretation, and tourist orientation in new settings. Such an analysis of the above four areas of concern will not of course be comprehensive. One needs to appreciate conflict and division theory and the political use of scientific research to appreciate fully the ongoing processes at work in the tourism–environment debate. However, an analysis of tourists' views of the environmental settings will hopefully serve as one useful input into this controversial area of concern.

Conceptions of tourist environments

In Chapter 2 it was argued that the concept of tourist may be usefully defined in experiential terms. Accordingly, any environment which fosters the feeling of being a tourist is a tourist environment. Such environments can exist either in one's home town or the other side of the world, provided they engender the necessary feelings associated with the tourist role. In general terms tourist environments will have high transient populations, a number of physical modifications to facilitate the inspection of the locale, and an inherent structure to control visitor accessibility. Such settings will create the transitory, insulated from danger, voyeuristic, occasionally exploitative, souvenir mentality identified earlier as characterizing the tourist experience. Practically any environment can, therefore, serve as a setting for tourist experiences. The ruins at Macchu Picchu, the night clubs at Acapulco, the harsh deserts of the Arab world, the sewers of Paris and the remnants of Auschwitz are all tourist environments.

Some tourist settings are, of course, infinitely more popular than others. Such settings undoubtedly fulfil the more common travel motivations of large numbers of people. The meaningfulness of popularity figures will depend on the size and capacity of the tourist setting studied. In this context it is convenient to use a hierarchical model to order tourist areas. For example, one can conceptualize whole countries and continents as tourist destinations. At a slightly less general level there are regional and local area images of tourist settings. Another step down in the hierarchy leads to an analysis of particular sites, cities or natural features. A fourth specific level of tourist environments may also be identified. This consists of the interiors of buildings, scenic vantage points and other small-scale areas with high tourist usage.

On the international level, for example, Spain is clearly one of the world's most popular destinations (Robinson, 1976; Waters, 1979, 1980). The fact that such popularity in current estimates places the total number of visitors at 30–35 million a year, and has been achieved in a 20-year period, represents a remarkable display of the combined forces of economics and imitation in shaping tourist traffic (Williams and Zelinsky, 1970; Cosgrove and Jackson, 1972). Most countries have specialized regions where seasonal tourist figures can be staggeringly high. It has been estimated that the Southwest of England, principally Devon and Cornwall, receives 5 million visitors in the months of July and August (BTA, 1980).

The concentration of tourists becomes even more apparent when the visitor statistics are examined on a smaller scale. In any one year major tourist cities of the world (e.g. London, New York, Paris, Amsterdam, Rome) receive visitor totals of at least half of their resident population. Thus London with some 8 or so million tourists per annum is to the fore in the visitor count, but all major cities have been forced to develop tourist hotel enclaves and regions of specialization to cope with such a volume of visitors. Specific tourist sites may in one year see the equivalent of the population of a major international city go through their doors. For example, the Tower of London was visited by over 3 million people in 1978 (BTA, 1978). Such high attendance figures are not confined to major city tourist attractions. In 1978

Stonehenge in Salisbury received 795,000 visitors while the Roman Baths at Bath was visited by 793,700 people. There are, no doubt, other sites (e.g. Lenin's tomb, the Taj Mahal, the Great Wall of China) with equally impressive visitor statistics, but the point which can be made from the British data is applicable throughout; tourists seek out highly specialized and experientially important environments in vast numbers. These environments are the most obvious, problematic and visible tourist environments which a social psychological approach to the topic must seek to understand.

Geographical approaches based both on the objective classification of destination features and the subjective appraisal by tourists of destinations have already been mentioned in Chapter 1. Such investigations of the perceived image of holiday destination areas tends to lead to piecemeal research with few general integrative findings. A more conceptually sophisticated approach which offers the possibility of cross-situational integration is that of Cohen (1979) who, as outlined in Chapter 1, has postulated a four-category model of tourist space. This model is organized according to two variables; one, the tourists' impression of the scene as real or staged; and two, the nature of the scene itself as real or staged. This 2×2 classification gives rise to four possible tourist–environment experiences; authenticity which is recognized and correctly perceived, tourist questioning of authenticity when it is in fact real, tourist failure to recognize a contrived space and tourist recognition of the created, manufactured environment. This four-fold division of tourist space may usefully be expanded by adding a third dimension, that of the tourists' desire for or indifference to authenticity. This important variable may be seen as moderating tourist satisfaction. For example, consider tourists whose impression of the tourist scene is that it is staged, and the reality is that the scene is a staged one. For those tourists who desire authenticity it is probable that this correct perception of the tourist environment as set up or structured to please tourists will attenuate their satisfaction with the site whereas tourists who are indifferent to the authenticity of environments may be considerably content with the same locale. This third variable has the effect of creating two figures to describe tourist–environment relationships; one figure for each of the two tourist types proposed (see Figure 5.1). How might such a classification of tourist space be useful for our understanding of tourist environments?

There are four sources of utility and strength in the above approach. First, the approach is conceived at the right level of generality for understanding an international phenomenon. It is a cross-situational approach which is not derived from or limited to any local or specific national analysis. It is appropriate to most levels of the hierarchy of tourist environments outlined earlier, but is particularly useful for specific tourist site analysis. It considers both the human and the environmental influence in tourist–environment interaction and emphasizes that the integration of these forces is effected in the

(1) Tourists with a high need for authenticity

Tourists' impression of scene

		Real	Staged
Nature of scene	Real	Authentic and recognized. High satisfaction	Suspicion of staging. Low satisfaction
	Staged	Failure to recognize. High satisfaction	Inauthenticity recognized. Low satisfaction

(2) Tourists with a low need for authenticity

Tourists' impression of scene

		Real	Staged
Nature of scene	Real	Authenticity recognized. Moderately high satisfaction	Suspicion of staging. Moderate satisfaction
	Staged	Failure to recognize. Moderately high satisfaction	Inauthenticity recognized. High satisfaction

FIG. 5.1   A two-way model of tourist–environment authenticity (after Cohen, 1979).

phenomenological reality of the individual. The approach can be considered to be a theoretically embedded one because it builds on a tradition of social-psychological enquiry concerned with self-presentation. The work of Goffman (1959) emphasized that a dramaturgical metaphor emphasizing on-stage or front- and back-stage performance is helpful in understanding overt social behaviour designed for others as opposed to behaviour for more private, limited audiences. Development of this notion has led to some insight in non-verbal behaviour (such as lying) and the nature of the self concept (Wylie, 1974). Such fields of enquiry are not directly related to tourist–environment relationships but the existence of a parallel literature in other fields based on a similar starting point or model affords a resource for record enquiry. It is in this way that the authenticity model of tourist–environment interaction may be said to be embedded in research literature. An analogy here is the area of social skills research which has emerged as a major applied field of social psychology. This area has built on a model of motor skills which provided initial theoretical guidance and some useful analogies for exploring the area of interest. Now, however, social skills is a major field in its own right with a credibility and utility which exceeds the original model of motor behaviour (Trower, Bryant and Argyle, 1978).

A totally manufactured tourist environment, Puerto de la Cruz, Tenerife.

The authenticity model also adds a very clear cognitive, attributional component to the theme of man–environment interaction. This may be contrasted with an approach such as that adopted by Mehrabian and Russell (1974) which conceives environments as having predominantly emotional impacts such as eliciting states of pleasure, arousal and dominance. While these components have proved to be useful in describing leisure environments—Mehrabian and Russell demonstrated that the desire to stay in a leisure-type setting was positively correlated only with the pleasure dimension—it is clear that at least a fourth variable which is cognitive is necessary to add completion to their scheme. By way of example, a tourist environment such as Disneyworld, Florida, may provide the visitor with high scores on the pleasure, arousal and dominance dimensions. However, if many tourists see the environment as structured and inauthentic and dislike these sorts of settings, then the cognitive interpretation of the experience become a critical one.

Further, the authenticity model is sufficiently explicit to provide testable predictions concerning tourist–environment interaction. This quality of specificity is surely needed in the area of man–environment interactions. Cohen (1979) has suggested for example that tourists who expect inauthenticity and find it (cell 4 of the model) will still be quite satisfied with their destination. On the other hand tourists who demand authenticity, who visit a structured inauthentic environment and perceive that environment as inauthentic will be dissatisfied with their holiday setting. Development and refinement of this approach could produce studies of the same tourists in settings of different authenticity as well as studies of tourists seeking differing degrees of authenticity responding to the same setting. It would also be of interest to explore the deviation of tourists' needs for authenticity as well as the major physical environmental proofs which act as cues to authentic and inauthentic settings.

The authenticity model also suggests another way of exploring a difficult problem in tourist research, that of measuring tourist satisfaction. Studies such as those by Pizam, Yoram and Arie (1978) have tended to show that tourist satisfaction is a multi-faceted concept which subdivides into a number of independent factors. One can suggest that satisfaction with the authenticity of the tourist environment may be one of the overarching factors which subsumes many of the more specific components of other satisfaction measures (such as accommodation facilities, extent of commercialization and beach opportunities). Again, the authenticity approach suggest insights into the tourist–environment relationship which await empirical support. It is of course disappointing to report that the research to substantiate this approach has not yet been conducted. In Chapter 6 of this book, some preliminary evidence from an international survey of tourists, very positive and very negative experiences will be shown to be consistent with some hypotheses derived from this approach.

As well as outlining one conceptualization of tourist environments which promises to stimulate and guide future research, this chapter seeks to review the small number of studies which have looked at changed attitudes to the environment consequent on travelling to that environment.

Attitude change to tourist environments

A host of studies both in environmental perception and the tourist literature have been concerned with the image of, or attitude towards, far-distant places. A sampling of these tourist studies produces work such as studies of the perceived tourist potential of an area (Georgulas, 1970; Mayo, 1973; Hunt, 1975; Swart, Gearing and Var, 1976; and Walker, 1976). Geographers, too, have been concerned with the images of far-distant places with studies ranging from the images of schoolchildren (Haddon, 1960) through cognitive mapping approaches (Whittaker, 1972; Saarinen, 1973; Downs and Stea, 1977) to multivariate analyses of destination images obtained through repertory grids (Harrison and Sarre, 1971; Riley and Palmer, 1976). Very few studies have investigated changes in environmental images either as a direct research goal or even as a reliability check on their image data.

However, a real concern of a social psychological account of tourist–environment relationships must lie in the issue of whether tourist experience in an environment engenders mental souvenirs, that is changed images and conceptions of the place, as a consequence of the visit. There is considerable tangential and anecdotal evidence that experience of a new environment should affect travellers' attitudes to that area. As the travelling hero of the 1960s Jack Kerouac expressed it: "Of course world travel isn't as good as it seems, it's only after you've come back from all the heat and horror . . . you remember the weird scenes you saw" (Kerouac (1960) pp. 136–7). The notion that travel can change attitudes and beliefs is an implicit assumption both in the tourist literature and in many prestigious international fellowships and grants.

It is necessary here to reflect on what is meant by the term "attitude change". This expression can most usefully be interpreted as a change of at least limited duration of the polarity of the tourists' evaluation of a physical setting. This definition borrows from the attitude literature and conceptual underpinnings of Fishbein and Aszen (1975), while stressing that the changed evaluation must last beyond the more ephemeral mood changes directly associated with the environmental experience itself.

A study conducted by the author (Pearce, 1981) fulfils these requirements for environmental attitude change in relation to young package-tourists holidaying in Greece and Morocco. The concerns of the study may be summarized as follows. It used the repertory grid technique to assess tourists' perceptions of foreign countries as holiday destinations and explored a limited aspect of the hypothesis that travel "broadens the mind" by investigating whether or not a small sample of tourists when studied in detail showed attitudinal and perceptual changes towards the country visited. It also tested the hypothesis that there is a generalization effect in tourists' attitudinal changes. This proposal suggested that if attitudinal changes occurred between the pre- and post-travel assessments of the visited country, then smaller but similar changes would take place in the tourists' attitudes towards similar holiday environments.

Three groups of British subjects were used in the study. Two of these groups were tourist groups, and the third was a sample of control subjects. There were 41 travellers to Morocco, 31 travellers to Greece, and 25 control subjects. The destinations of Morocco and Greece were chosen for study since two different destinations were needed to test the generalization hypothesis.

Twenty-two travellers, 11 destined for Morocco and 11 for Greece, were obtained from the bookings lists of the Jet-Trek Company. The average age was 22 years; range 19–25. There were 12 males and 10 females in the group. The remaining travellers to each country were obtained from privately organized parties using the same kinds of transport and travel arrangements.

The control subjects, 12 males and 13 females, were obtained from the private organizations. They were those members of the same groups who could not join these particular expeditions. They were matched with the travelling groups for sex, social class, educational level and interest in travel. The age of the controls and the travellers from the private organizations was slightly less (18 years, range 16–20) than that of the travel company groups.

The task administered to the 97 subjects consisted of a 7 × 13 grid. A rating scale accompanied the grid. Subjects were asked to fill in the grid by rating seven elements on the 13 constructs. A set of detailed sorting and checking procedures was used to select 13 constructs for the environmental appraisal of the seven countries. These techniques insured that the constructs were relevant and natural from the perspective of the tourists.

The choice of elements in the study was made as follows. Seven holiday environments were selected by the writer. Two of these, Greece and Morocco, were considered to be the target countries; that is, they were the countries which must be examined in order to test the change hypothesis. The traveller's country of departure, Britain, was included since it has been suggested that travelling abroad can affect one's attitude to one's home environment (Useem and Useem, 1967). The remaining four holiday environments were selected in an attempt to test the generalization hypothesis. This hypothesis demands that attitudes towards both dissimilar and similar holiday environments be obtained since a generalization of attitude change is predicted for similar environments but not for dissimilar ones. Specifically, the holiday environments of Iceland and Switzerland were selected as dissimilar environments to those of Greece and Morocco. The generalization hypothesis suggests that there will be little carry-over in perception to these environments as a consequence of having visited Greece and Morocco. The two environments selected as similar environments to the target ones were Tunisia (as a similar environment to Morocco) and Italy (for Greece).

The timing and administration of the questionnaires

It can be suggested that the results of any study of intercultural contact should be linked to the phases of culture adjustment proposed by Gullahorn and Gullahorn (1963). It follows that the administration of a questionnaire should also consider this point and should systematically seek to obtain responses from all subjects at the same time. Owing to some assistance from the organizers of the various travel parties it was possible to test all groups exactly 1 week before their departure and one can reasonably suggest that this timing is sufficiently removed from the holiday itself and the phases of intercultural adjustment to allow the tourist to give a considered appraisal of his forthcoming or his completed holiday. A file of political and world events was kept during the course of the study to ensure that any changes in the tourists' perceptions were due to his holiday and not to international hostilities. No events occurred which directly impinged on the study.

The results for the change hypothesis and for the generalization hypothesis

The group changes in the travellers' perceptions of the holiday environments were analysed by taking the consensus grids for the post-travel responses from the consensus grids for the pre-travel responses. This involved the use of the Delta program (Slater, 1972), which computes the major components of the resulting difference grid.

The essential information from the Delta grids is presented in Figures 5.3–5.5. It should be emphasized that the details reported below represent the main *differences* between the pre- and post-travel grids. Following the conventions outlined by Slater (1972), the constructs are represented as direction lines in the construct space. The distance of the elements from the origin may be taken as the change effect due to travelling plus the changes due to noise effects in the testing material. The relative insignificance of these noise effects is demonstrated in a later figure by examining the changes for the control subjects. Before considering the findings in detail it is important to

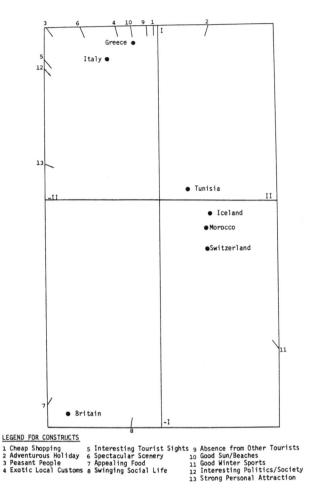

LEGEND FOR CONSTRUCTS

1 Cheap Shopping	5 Interesting Tourist Sights	9 Absence from Other Tourists
2 Adventurous Holiday	6 Spectacular Scenery	10 Good Sun/Beaches
3 Peasant People	7 Appealing Food	11 Good Winter Sports
4 Exotic Local Customs	8 Swinging Social Life	12 Interesting Politics/Society
		13 Strong Personal Attraction

FIG. 5.3   The loadings of the elements in construct space on the two major components of the Delta (post-travel minus pre-travel) grid for the travellers to Greece.

document the amount or extent of the change of the travellers' post-travel impressions. This may be conveniently summarized by a percentage deviation from the pre-travel act of impresssions. Information from the Delta analysis enabled a percentage deviation to be calculated for each travel group. For the travellers to Morocco the post-travel grid represents a 21 per cent overall change from the pre-travel scores, while for the travellers to Greece the figure is 31 per cent and for the non-travel control group the change is 11 per cent. Accordingly it can be suggested that the degree of change for the traveller groups is greater than that due to test–retest considerations of other effects as measured by the control group. The detailed findings of the analysis will now be considered.

The point to note in Figure 5.3 is that two components of change account for a very substantial proportion of the variance (over 90 per cent) and that the elements which change most are those of Italy, Greece and Britain. Following the travellers' holidays to Greece, Greece and Italy are seen as more adventurous holiday destinations. They are also seen as having cheaper shopping, fewer tourists, more exotic customs, more peasant people and more spectacular scenery. Britain, on the other hand, is seen as at the other end of this dimension; that is less adventurous and more expensive. However, the tourists do come to see their own country as having more appealing food and of being somewhat better for social life than they did prior to their holiday experiences.

Some additional information provided by the Delta printout which summarizes the changes in an element as a percentage of the total grid change highlights the significance of the three elements discussed above. The results were Britain (39·5 per cent), Greece (22·5 per cent), Morocco (3·3 per cent), Italy (21·0 per cent), Iceland (3·6 per cent), Switzerland (7·7 per cent) and Tunisia (2·1 per cent). The relevance of all these results to the change and generalization hypotheses is as follows. Change certainly does occur with respect to the target element (Greece) and this change also generalizes to other elements (e.g. Britain and Italy).

The information concerning the changes in the Moroccan travellers' perceptions of the visited holiday environments will now be outlined. Again both the component loadings for the Delta grid and a plot of these loadings in two dimensions will be provided. This material is presented in Figure 5.4.

The most important supplementary information to Figure 5.4 is that the two components of change account for a substantial proportion of the variance (nearly 70 per cent) and that the elements which change most are Morocco, Britain and Tunisia. Following the travellers' holidays to Morocco, Morocco and Tunisia are seen as having more peasants, being more adventurous holiday environments, having cheaper shopping, more tourist sights and more spectacular scenery. Britain, Greece and Italy are seen as lacking these attributes but Britain is seen by the returning tourists as having more appealing food. The information provided by the Delta printout which summarizes the changes in any element as a percentage of the total grid changes provides important information. The results were Britain (20·5 per cent), Greece (11·8 per cent), Morocco (26·6 per cent), Italy (10·7 per cent), Iceland (12·2 per cent), Switzerland (4·5 per cent) and Tunisia (13·4 per cent).

The information concerning the control group of travellers will now be outlined. This material helps us to understand the "noise" in the data for the two travel groups. To demonstrate the relative insignificance of these noise

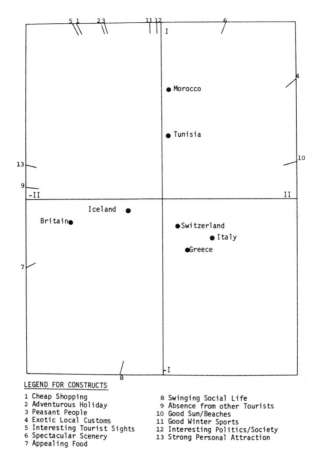

LEGEND FOR CONSTRUCTS

1 Cheap Shopping	8 Swinging Social Life
2 Adventurous Holiday	9 Absence from other Tourists
3 Peasant People	10 Good Sun/Beaches
4 Exotic Local Customs	11 Good Winter Sports
5 Interesting Tourist Sights	12 Interesting Politics/Society
6 Spectacular Scenery	13 Strong Personal Attraction
7 Appealing Food	

FIG. 5.4   The loadings of the elements in construct space on the two major components of the Delta (post-travel minus pre-travel) grid for the travellers to Morocco.

effects the same information as that presented for the travel groups—namely the percentage of the variance accounted for by the components, the component loadings and a plot of the first two components—will be outlined and compared with the results for the travel groups. This material is presented in Figure 5.5.

An important factor which should be noted when interpreting Figure 5.5 is that in this instance, unlike the preceding two occasions, the Delta grid represents the difference between two consensus grids, which are highly intercorrelated (0·944). That is, we are dealing with a smaller change than on the previous two occasions. Hence any changes in elements and constructs for this Delta grid are of less significance than for the travel groups. The two

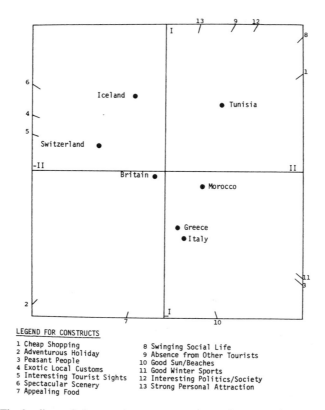

FIG. 5.5   The loadings of elements in construct space on the two major components of the
Delta (post-travel minus pre-travel) grid for the control subjects.

components represented in Figure 5.5 comprise 66 per cent of the variance. The main finding for the control subjects is that after their "non-travel" month in Britain they see Greece and Italy as having more sun and beaches than before and also having more appealing food. It is particularly note-worthy that Britain, one of the major elements to change for the travel groups, undergoes almost no change whatsoever for the control group. The other changes can be interpreted as a fairly random scattering of elements and constructs. Most importantly the pattern of loadings on the compo-nents, including the example above, does not parallel the pattern for either of the travel groups.

The Delta printout provided the following details concerning the changes for each element as a percentage of the total grid change: Britain (6·3 per cent), Greece (14·4 per cent), Morocco (9·4 per cent), Italy (15·7 per cent), Iceland (21·0 per cent), Switzerland (12·7 per cent), Tunisia (20·2 per cent). Again the kinds of changes are *unrelated* to those seen for the two travel groups both in terms of the elements which change and the gradients of the amount of change, thus justifying the assertion that the effects reported for the other two groups are due to travelling, not test variability or changes resulting from intervening international events. The results obtained in the preceding section support the change hypothesis, which was one of the two main hypotheses of this study. In particular it was shown that two tourist groups—one visiting Greece, the other visiting Morocco—changed some of their perceptions of these countries as holiday environments. The travellers to Greece saw that holiday environment as more adventurous, better for cheap shopping and freer from other tourists than they did prior to their travels. These results support the general form of the change hypothesis as outlined in the introductory section. The travellers to Morocco saw it as more adventurous, better for cheap shopping, having more interesting tourist sights and bringing them into contact with more peasant people than they did prior to their holiday. These results also support the general form of the change hypothesis. It seems that specific tourist groups can change their perceptions of the visiting country as a consequence of travelling.

The evidence relating to the generalization hypothesis allows us to support the broad outline of the hypothesis. This can be explained in detail for each travel group as follows. For Greek travellers it was shown that generalization, which was defined as a spread of change in perception from the target environment to similar environments, did occur (see Figure 5.3 and associated comments). The greatest changes occurred for the environments of Britain and Italy.

It seems that the perception of one's home environment may be significantly altered by the travellers' holiday. However, this change in the perception of the home environment seems to be independent of any similarity to the target environment. Indeed, the tourists' perception of the home environment may exhibit greater change than the visited environment. This is the case in the present study of the Greek travellers where the changes in the element Britain account for 34 per cent of the total changes in the grid; changes in the perception of Greece accounted for 22 per cent of the total change. There seems to be an important anchor or contrast effect with regard to the home environment which warrants further investigation (cf. Helson, 1948).

For the Moroccan travellers it was again shown that generalization does occur. It was predicted that the greatest change would occur with respect to Tunisia. The greatest change occurred with respect to Britain, Tunisia and Iceland. Again it is apparent that the importance of one's home country is underlined. The changes in Tunisia are in agreement with the selection of that environment as a similar location to Morocco by the writer. The reported change with respect to Iceland may indicate that there are more similarities to Morocco (e.g. remoteness from Britain, exciting destination) than was originally envisaged.

In conclusion one can suggest that tourists can change their perception of the holiday environment they visit. Furthermore, the perceptual changes which occur may not be limited to the visited locality but may reflect back on one's home country and on occasions to other holiday environments which are generally recognized as similar to the one which has recently been visited.

Finally, this study has illustrated the application of the Kelly grid technique to tourists' view of holiday locations. It has shown empirically that small groups of tourists travelling together can change their images of visited locations. Clearly the research presented uses a very select sample of tourists and the image changes of other styles and groups of tourists may bear little relation to the present findings. However, this study indicates that the time has come in tourist research when speculation about tourists' impressions of places should be replaced by measurement and testing of any attitudinal changes from the tourists' own perspectives.

A number of other studies have also demonstrated the effects of travel on environmental images and perceptions. For example, Sonnenfeld (1967) studied the perceptions of Alaska held by groups with differing contact with that environment. This result can be broadly summarized by the finding that the more non-Alaskan Americans travelled within the Alaskan environment the more they appreciated its rugged scenery and features. He also discovered that a small group of Alaskan Indians who have travelled to Hawaii and other parts of the United States were quite favourably disposed to exotic tropical and beach environments. For both groups, increased familiarity and travel contact with a novel environment promoted an enhanced evaluation of that environment.

Travelling to unfamiliar environments has been shown to affect not just the evaluation of landscape and scenery, but the images of the visited cities. Pearce *et al.* (1981) investigated student stereotypes of Australian capital cities. They demonstrated that students who had travelled more had more differentiated and less stereotyped view of interstate cities. The correlation between the amount of student travel and the extent of student stereotyping of the cities was 0·83. In this particular study it was noticeable that students living in the more remote states of Australia (Western Australia and Tasmania) drew fewer distinctions among the Australian cities but did so with a higher level of agreement and stereotyping than their better-travelled student colleagues from other states (see Table 5.1).

The issue of changing attitudes and images of environments through positive travel experience is of wide-ranging significance. As outlined in Chapter 4, there are a number of organizations and individuals who have argued that the right sorts of travel experiences can foster harmonious international relationship and sympathetic environmental awareness. As a consequence of the travel contact experience some individuals are motivated to political

TABLE 5.1 *Stereotyping scores as indicated by the percentage of modal responses for students from Australian cities (after Pearce et al., 1981)*

Viewed city	Viewing city*						Mean percentages
	Adelaide	Brisbane	Hobart	Melbourne	Perth	Sydney	
Adelaide	39	41	43	40	46	39	41·2
Brisbane	49	37	48	41	38	35	41·3
Hobart	50	43	44	49	51	43	46·6
Melbourne	46	37	58	42	48	38	44·8
Perth	45	44	44	41	43	44	43·5
Sydney	40	44	43	42	42	41	41·8
Mean percentages	44·5	41·0	46·7	42·5	44·7	40·0	

* The students who had travelled most were in order: Melbourne, Sydney, Brisbane, Adelaide, Hobart and Perth.

action in issues of human rights and international and environmental concerns (Hiller, 1976). Such concern for other people and other environments can be seen to represent an ideal in terms of the much-vaunted claims that travel develops an international perspective in world affairs. Unfortunately, adequate documentation of such international effects of attitude change associated with travel is still rather limited. While such effects may be poorly documented, they are consistent with Lundberg's (1973) model of objective and emotional distance. Using an information-processing analogy and formula, Lundberg demonstrated that Swedish subjects were more emotionally concerned with phenomena which were subjectively close to their home environment. More precisely the emotional distance was found to be inversely proportional to the square root of the estimated or subjective distance (Lundberg, 1973). A number of specific empirical studies (Ekman and Bratfisch, 1965; Dornic, 1967; Bratfisch, 1969) provided evidence for this form of the relationship in other countries and with different methods.

For the present purposes, international travel can be viewed as one of the forces shrinking the subjective distance between the observer and international events, thus increasing the emotional impact of such phenomena. For example, the impacts of war, terrorist attacks and natural disasters are much more powerful and immediate when the observer can link the news item to his own travel experience in that specific environment.

Environmental interpretation and orientation

It was argued in the previous chapter that many tourists do not come into direct contact with their hosts. This was demonstrated to be particularly applicable to tourist–host encounters involving language difficulties and marked cultural differences. Similarly, there is a set of barriers and interpretive mechanisms interposed between tourists and some of the environments they seek to explore. The most obvious of these controls involve the use of physical barriers, off-limit areas and the limited development of site facilities to prevent heavy tourist use. Sometimes there are conscious management plans to control visitor damage (Cohen, 1978) or to preserve the privacy of residents in a tourist area (Bosselman, 1978). This area of enquiry falls largely into the planning and design field of environmental studies (Sharpe, 1976). It is useful to note that the planning studies are really an intuitively derived set of programmatic recommendations for both controlling visitors and letting them experience the environment. They are not, as yet, tied to any model of visitor–environment interaction.

One can reflect here on the way in which the model of tourist–environmental authenticity could be applied to the field of managing environments. It immediately focuses interest on three issues; the visitors' need for authenticity and contact with the environment, the unique and authentic features of that environment and the interface between the tourist and environmental setting, which is necessary to achieve the kind of experience the tourist seeks, while preserving the setting for others. If one takes these three criteria into account, then debates about the relative merits of communication and interpretive aids fall into perspective. It is not simply a matter of whether signposts and charts are better than brochures, or whether a ranger's presence is superior to portable personal cassettes, but rather the relative advantages and disadvantages of the strategies as they relate to the aspects of the authenticity model. This focuses attention on the role of the interpretive aid as a factor fitting the visitor's need for authenticity, its usefulness in presenting the setting and its influence on the quality of the experience offered while conserving the environment.

A small-scale study in the specific context of tourist caves in Northern Australia illustrates some of the advantages of using this authenticity framework to examine management issues. In a 2-year study of visitors to the fragile limestone caves at Chillagoe, North Queensland, the author established that the visitors expected to encounter a set of environments which had been changed very little by human discovery and contact. The visitors' experiences in this setting tended to confirm their expectation that the environment was little altered by the cave management authority. Major factors which served to confirm the visitors' authenticity expectations were unobtrusive lighting fittings, unsurfaced cave paths, no special-coloured lighting of cave features, few signs of cave damage by other tourists, and the use of magnesium flares and hand-held lights in the bigger cave because a full network of lighting had not been established. Visitors were highly satisfied with the caves as an attractive unique environment and reacted positively to all guided tours, which lasted for up to 3 hours. In this example visitor motives and notions of authenticity were being met. There was a fortuitous meshing of the person–environment interface because the visitor seeking authenticity was able to experience authenticity. It can be suggested that such a marriage of motives and expectations promotes satisfaction. This suggestion parallels the work outlined on tourist–host attitudes which may be seen as due to initial favourability and holiday satisfaction as outlined in the previous chapter (Pearce, 1980).

Another illustration of the authenticity perspective on tourist–environment debate lies in the study of visitors to special environments of historical and cultural interest. An interesting study of such environments is the work of the English Tourist Board considering the role of tourism in relation to the preservation and conservation of the country's great cathedrals. In this situation the integration between people and the environments they come to visit does not function quite as smoothly as in the example of the remote Northern Australian caves. It is apparent, for instance, that while many visitors seek to understand and admire the cathedrals for their artistic, cultural and historical value, the clergy and support staff who work in these medieval masterpieces emphasize both the spiritual and cultural experiences available in this setting. The Dean of Ripon, for instance, stated "We give complete priority to the sense of worship" (English Tourist Board (1979), Foreword). The authenticity model serves to stress that the on-site experience of the tourist is altered by the current religious functions of the cathedrals. What the tourist seeks in this situation is not fully available due to the competing contemporary functions of the environment. The clergy and management councils of the churches can be seen to be in a double-bind situation. For financial reasons they must continue to preserve the tourist trade. This depends on the cathedrals functioning as unaltered, living spiritual museums. Yet, since the tourists distance the services, tourist barriers and controls must be introduced. The use of such barriers may frustrate and alienate some of the cathedral visitors.

These two examples of special environments may be usefully compared. One situation works exceedingly well because the very remoteness of the natural environment in question serves to select and filter out all those people who are not genuinely interested in that setting. Further, the quality and kind of experience offered in the cave environments are relatively well defined. Since the caves have been disturbed only marginally the matching of visitor expectations and available environmental experiences is successful. For the cathedrals, however, there are few filters which control visitor access to the environments. This is particularly true of Westminster Abbey and Canterbury Cathedral. Furthermore, the available experience offered in the cathedral environment is not well defined. At present, the failure to fit the motives and expectations of the visitors to the experiences offered in that environment are not proving too severe in the cathedral settings. However, as the costs of environmental damage escalate, it is apparent that a more precise matching of people and the environment will be needed to reduce mutual friction. Dissatisfied and bored tourists, one can suggest, are more likely to damage the visited environment. Already the maintenance of the cathedrals is financially difficult. An increase in maintenance costs due to tourist damage would be alarming.

It is highly likely that the future of cathedrals and tourism will rest on a publicity campaign designed not so much to encourage all tourists but to select the right kinds of cathedral visitors. In addition to an attempt to appeal to selected audiences cathedrals will need to develop their educational and interpretive facilities, while bearing in mind that intrusive signs of tourist management will destroy the very authenticity many visitors seek.

Maps and orientation

Most tourist environments, whether they are caves, open areas, museums or cathedrals, present visitors with problems of orientation and finding the way. It has been argued that many visitors to museums and displays prefer not to ask attendants for directions, but will consult such personnel on topics such as the content of the display (Bell, Fisher and Loomis, 1978). It can be suggested that the reluctance to seek orientation information stems from the tourist's desire not to appear foolish and overly dependent. Given the consistent finding that disorientation is highly emotionally arousing and unpleasant (Lynch, 1960), it would appear that visitors who do not seek orientation information are strongly motivated by their desire not to appear as a typical or average tourist. In Goffman's terminology, there is strong tendency for tourists to role-distance themselves from other tourists by establishing their own orientation in the visited environment (cf. Goffman, 1959). It is apparent therefore that tourist maps should be readily available to a wide range of tourists and should be able to be used without reference to supporting personnel.

The topic of orientation and map-reading in relation to tourists' needs and uses has received some attention from psychologists. Perhaps the most practical contribution to this topic has been the specific tourist maps of Durham, York and Newcastle-Upon-Tyne produced by Fisher (1974, 1975, 1976).

Fisher argued that conventional city or tourist maps, which are accurate in terms of scale and detail, fail to serve tourists' perceptual and orientation needs. By asking several hundred people questions concerning landmarks, routes and perceived distances in the city, he generated maps which took into account human distortion of the environment. These maps, which resemble an aerial photograph in a line-drawn format, contain many distortions of space and distance but the researchers argued that these errors mirror the people's impressions of the environment. Considerable claims are made for these maps. For example, it has been suggested that perceptual maps are ten times more effective than cartographic maps when one compares the speed of identifying landmarks and of finding one's way (Fisher, 1975). In addition, since perceptual maps omit much detailed information and highlight important city landmarks in a three-dimensional projection, it is probable that they have considerable aesthetic appeal to tourists. This in turn may promote their use and assist tourists' way-finding through more frequent map consultation. Until more systematic research is available on the efficacy of perceptual maps, such claims must be treated with considerable caution.

There have been other calls to study maps from the user's as opposed to the specialist's perspective. For example, Bronzaft, Dobrow and O'Hanlon (1976) analysed the adequacy of the New York subway maps by testing the ability of riders to use the system and reach set destinations with minimum fuss. They argue that their study is one of the first to "introduce the concept of testing orientational aids with their potential users" (p. 581). Less than one half of their subjects followed trip patterns which were "acceptable"— that is economical in time, money and effort—and the researchers suggest

FIG. 5.6   The supermap of York (Reproduced by permission of Gerald H. Fisher, Department of Psychology, University of Newcastle upon Tyne)

further work should be directed at how to design maps and other orientation aids from the user's perspective.

Attempts to evaluate the properties of maps has often degenerated into a piecemeal approach. For example there are numerous investigations of the specific components of cartographic assembly. Bartz (1969, 1970) has demonstrated the advantages of typographic legibility while the use of colour, statistical symbols, and line weight have been studied by Cuff (1973) and Wright (1967). There are two levels of inadequacy in this approach. The integration of the parts may well change their interpretation when they are viewed as a *Gestalt*. Secondly, maps have particular functions and are designed for specific target populations. It is unlikely, at least on an *a priori* basis, that the features which aid the use and comprehension of maps for one population of users (such as tourists) will adequately serve a second group (e.g., town planners). This implies that map evaluation must (a) consider the total integration of map information rather than assessing component parts, and (b) evaluate maps for specific target populations separately.

In addition to considerations concerning the quality and type of map tourists use, any understanding of tourist orientation must consider human cognitive mapping ability. This ability may be conveniently thought of as the mental organization and synthesis of orientation information. As yet, little attention has been directed towards the cognitive maps of tourists, and how these maps develop. Lynch (1960) argued that tourists, unlike residents, initially rely on landmarks for orientation. In time, as the cognitive map of the tourist develops, more paths (streets, routes and tracks) are integrated into the total schema. While this suggestion has intuitive appeal, it has not been confirmed in empirical studies. For example, Pearce (1977) collected sketch maps from young, predominantly American, tourists visiting Oxford. He found that tourists who had been in the city 6 days were not using different elements of the city to orientate themselves more than did tourists who had been in the University area for 2 days. Perhaps the period of time in the city was not adequate to test fully Lynch's proposed "switch-over" from landmarks to paths. This remains an unsettled point. Its resolution will be of interest to tourist map designers because one can suggest that the proportion of landmarks–paths in perceptual maps (cf. Fisher, 1975) should reflect the landmarks–paths proportions and use demonstrated in tourists' mental maps.

Reid (1980), following the work of Appleyard, Lynch and Meyer (1964) and Carr and Schissler (1969), has argued that attention must also be given to the tourists' predominant mode of transport when considering cognitive mapping ability and the design of maps. Working in two tourist cities of Northern Australia, Reid demonstrated that drivers and passengers remembered the routes and landmarks of the city differently. The specific effects obtained depended on whether the driver or passenger was actively involved in finding the way in the visited city. Drivers who self-directed, and passengers who directed drivers, were better oriented and remembered more paths than drivers who were directed by a passenger or passengers who played no part in the way-finding process.

There also appears to be a possibility that sex differences in cognitive mapping exist. Pearce (1977) found that while males and females were equally well oriented in the city, this result was achieved in different ways. Females tended to use more landmarks and districts in order to obtain the feel of the city while males utilized the street system and the angles between points to organize themselves spatially. This finding is consistent with sex differences in other visual–spatial cognitive tasks (Maccoby and Jacklin (1974) p. 92).

Undoubtedly, further individual differences in tourists' mapping ability and actual map use will be unearthed in future studies. The challenge for psychologists working in the area of cognitive mapping is to pinpoint for the cartographers not only the styles of maps which are best understood by users, but also the key individual and demographic variables which contribute to different way-finding skills. Knowledge of both of these areas of enquiry should assist in the construction of psychologically efficient tourist maps for specific client populations.

References

APPLEYARD, D., LYNCH, K. and MYER, J. (1964) *The View from the Road*. Cambridge, Mass.: MIT Press.

BARTZ, B. (1969) Type variation and the problem of cartographic type legibility. *Journal of Typographic Research*, **3**, 127–44.

BARTZ, B. (1970) Experimental use of the search task in an analysis of type legibility. *Cartographic Journal*, **7**, 103–12.

BELL, P. A., FISHER, J. D. and LOOMIS, R. J. (1978) *Environmental Psychology*. Philadelphia: W. B. Saunders.

BOSSELMAN, F. (1979) *In the Wake of the Tourist: Managing Special Places in Eight Countries*. Washington: The Conservation Foundation.

BRATFISCH, O. (1969) A further study of the relation between subjective distance and emotional involvement. *Acta Psychologica*, **29**, 244–55.

BRITISH TOURIST AUTHORITY (1978) *Digest of Tourist Statistics*, No. 8. London: British Tourist Authority.

BRITISH TOURIST AUTHORITY (1980) *Digest of Tourist Statistics*, No. 10. London: British Tourist Authority.

BRONZAFT, A., DOBROW, S. and O'HANLON, T. (1976) Spatial orientation in a subway system. *Environment and Behavior*, **8** (4), 575–94.

CAMPBELL, J. F. (1972) *Erosion and Accretion of Selected Hawaiian Beaches, 1962–1972*. Honolulu: The University of Hawaii Sea Grant Program.

CARR, S. and SCHISSLER, D. (1969) The city as a trip: perceptual selection and memory in the view from the road. *Environment and Behavior*, **1**, 7–36.

COHEN, E. (1978) The impact of tourism on the physical environment. *Annals of Tourism Research*, **2**, 215–37.

COHEN, E. (1979) Rethinking the sociology of tourism. *Annals of Tourism Research*, **6**, 18–35.

COSGROVE, I. and JACKSON, R. (1972) *The Geography of Recreation and Leisure*. London: Hutchinson University Library.

CUFF, D. (1973) Colour on temperature maps. *Cartographic Journal*, **10**, 17–21.

DORNIC, S. (1967) Subjective distance and emotional involvement: a verification of the exponent invariance. *Reports from the Psychological Laboratories*, Stockholm, **237**, 1–7.

DOWNS, R. M. and STEA, D. (1977) *Maps in Minds*. New York: Harper & Row.

EKMAN, G. and BRATFISCH, O. (1965) Subjective distance and emotional involvement; a psychological mechanism. *Acta Psychologica*, **24**, 446–53.

ENGLISH TOURIST BOARD (1979) *English Cathedrals and Tourism*. London: English Tourist Board.

EVANS, P. (1975) Perceptual maps. *New Behaviour*, 1 May.

FARRELL, B. H. (1977) *The Tourist Ghettos of Hawaii*. Santa Cruz: Center for South Pacific Studies, University of California.

FISHBEIN, M. and AJZEN, I. (1975) *Belief, Attitude, Intention and Behaviour: An Introduction to Theory and Research*. Reading, Mass.: Addison-Wesley.

FISHER, G. (1974) *The Perceptual Map of Newcastle-Upon-Tyne*. Newcastle-Upon-Tyne: Department of Psychology.

FISHER, G. (1975) *The Supermap of York*. Newcastle-Upon-Tyne: Department of Psychology.

FISHER, G. (1976) *The Perceptual Map of Durham*. Newcastle-Upon-Tyne: Department of Psychology.

GEORGULAS, N. (1970) Tourist destination features. *Journal of the Town Planning Institute*, **56** (10), 442–6.

GOFFMAN, E. (1959) *The Presentation of Self in Everyday Life*. New York: Doubleday.

GULLAHORN, J. E. and GULLAHORN, J. T. (1963) An extension of the U-curve hypothesis. *Journal of Social Issues*, **19**, 33–47,

HADDON, J. (1960) A view of foreign lands. *Geography*, **45**, 286–9.

HARRISON, J. and SARRE, P. (1971) Personal construct theory in the measurement of environmental images: problems and methods. *Environment and Behavior*, **3** (4), 351–74.

HELSON, H. (1948) Adaptation level as a basis for a quantitative theory of frames of reference. *Psychological Review*, **55**, 297–313.

HILLER, H. (1976) Some basic thoughts about the effects on tourism of changing values in receiving societies. *The Travel Research Association, Seventh Annual Conference Proceedings*, pp. 199–201.

HUNT, J. D. (1975) Image as a factor in tourism development. *Journal of Travel Research*, **13** (3), 1–8.

KEROUAC, J. (1972) *Lonesome Traveller*. London: Panther (first edition, 1960).

LUNDBERG, U. (1973) Emotional and geographical phenomena in psycho-physical research. In DOWNS, R. and STEA, D (eds) *Image and Environment*. London: Arnold.

LYNCH, K. (1960) *The Image of the City*. Cambridge, Mass.: MIT Press.

MACCOBY, E. E. and JACKLIN, N. W. (1974) *The Psychology of Sex Differences*. Stanford, Calif.: Stanford University Press.

MAYO, E. J. (1973) Regional images and regional travel behaviour. *The Travel Research Association, Fourth Annual Conference Proceedings*, pp. 211–18.

MEHRABIAN, A. and RUSSELL, J. A. (1974) *An Approach to Environmental Psychology*. Cambridge, Mass.: MIT Press.

MORRIS, D. (1979) *Animal Days*. London: Jonathan Cape.

NICHOLSON, M. (1972) Planned expansion of tourism to bring in new areas and fresh fields of interest. *Tourism and the Environment*, BTA, pp. 48–51.

PEARCE, P. L. (1977) Mental souvenirs: a study of tourists and their city maps. *Australian Journal of Psychology*, **29**, 203–10.

PEARCE, P. L. (1981) Perceived changes in holiday destinations: an illustrative study of the grid approach for tourists visiting Greece and Morocco. *Annals of Tourism Research*. (In press.)

PEARCE, P. L. (1981) The social and psychological effects of tourist–host contact. In BOCHNER, S. (ed.) *Studies in Cross-Cultural Interaction*. Oxford: Pergamon.

PEARCE, P., INNES, M., O'DRISCOLL, M. and MORSE, S. (1981) Stereotypes of Australian cities. *Australian Journal of Psychology*. (In press.)

PIZAM, A., YORAM, N. and ARIE, R. (1978) Dimensions of tourist satisfaction with a destination area. *Annals of Tourism Research*, **3**, 314–22.

REID, A. (1980) Passenger–Driver Differences in Recall of Two City Environments. Unpublished BA(Hons) thesis, James Cook University of North Queensland, Townsville, Australia.

RILEY, S. and PALMER, J. (1976) Of attitudes and latitudes: a repertory grid study of perceptions of seaside resorts. In SLATER, P. (ed.) *Explorations of Intrapersonal Space*. London: Wiley.

ROBINSON, H. (1976) *A Geography of Tourism*. London: Macdonald & Evans.

SAARINEN, T. F. (1973) Student views of the world. In DOWNS, R. and STEA, D. (eds) *Image and Environment*. London: Arnold.

SHARPE, G. (1976) *Interpreting the Environment*. New York: Wiley.

SINGH, T. V. (1979) On planning towns, tourism and environment. *Tourism Recreation Research*, **4** (2), 9–14.

SLATER, P. (1972) *Summary of the Output from DELTA*. London: Academic Department of Psychiatry, St George's Hospital.

SONNENFELD, J. (1967) Environmental perception and adaptation level in the Arctic. In LOWENTHAL, D. (ed.) *Environmental Perception and Behaviour*. Chicago: University of Chicago.

SWART, W. W., GEARING, C. and VAR, T. (1976) A simplified procedure for estimating the market attraction of a tourist area. *The Travel Research Association, Seventh Annual Conference Proceedings*, pp. 237–42.

TROWER, P., BRYANT, B. and ARGYLE, M. (1978) *Social Skills and Mental Health*. London: Methuen.

TURNER, L. and ASH, J. (1975) *The Golden Hordes*. London: Constable.

USEEM, J. and USEEM, R. The interfaces of a binational third culture; a study of the American community in India. *Journal of Social Issues*, **23**, 130–43.

WALKER, J. D. (1976) Using research to develop and test advertising for a destination . . . a case history. *The Travel Research Association, Seventh Annual Conference Proceedings*, pp. 171–4.

WATERS, S. R. (1979) *The Big Picture: Travel '79–'80, World Trends and Markets*. New York: ASTA Travel News.

WATERS, S. R. (1980) *The Big Picture: Travel '80–'81, World Trends and Markets*. New York: ASTA Travel News.

WHITTAKER, J. O. (1972) The country at the centre of the earth: a cross cultural study of ethnocentrism. In DAWSON, J. L. M. and LONNER, W. J. (eds) *Readings in Cross-Cultural Psychology*. Hong Kong University Press.

WILLIAMS, A. J. and ZELINSKY, W. (1970) On some patterns in international tourist flows. *Economic Geography*, **46** (4), 549–67.

WRIGHT, R. (1967) Selection of Line Weights for Solid Qualitative Line Symbols in Series on Maps. Unpublished Doctoral dissertation, University of Kansas.

WYLIE, R. C. (1974) *The Self-concept*, vol. 1, revised edition. Lincoln: University of Nebraska Press.

6

Inside the Tourists' Perspective

Introduction

Using a social psychological approach, the work discussed to date has been concerned with tourists' social roles, tourists' motivation for travelling, and tourists' reactions to the host nationality and novel environments. In these chapters it has been argued that more attention should be devoted to tourists' views of their travel experience.

Yet, despite the large number of studies reviewed, there has been little direct commentary or scope for considering comments from tourists themselves. The material reported in this chapter will illustrate the theoretical concerns of the preceding analyses by exploring a number of unstructured commentaries from a wide range of tourists.

The material presented in this chapter will be drawn mainly from 400 travel experiences or incidents provided by some 200 tourists in the United States, Europe, Canada and Australia. One can ask with some justification whether it was necessary to collect further tourist accounts of their travel experiences when there exists a considerable literature on tourist satisfaction and views of vacations (Hunt, 1975; Pizam *et al.*, 1978; Rubenstein, 1980). It was felt, however, that the existing material duplicated, at least in aim if not in detail, the more detailed analytic accounts of tourists' experiences presented in earlier chapters. Studies such as those by Rubenstein (1980) do offer interesting large-scale survey data on what Americans think about their holidays, but they provide limited opportunities for the tourists to express openly their views and interpretations of people, places, the tourist role, their own motivations and their reactions to travelling.

The data collected for the present chapter was obtained as follows. Bearing in mind the aim of the study which was to illustrate the qualitative aspects of tourist experiences, it was decided to obtain responses from a wide range of tourists who would be likely to have been involved in many different types of travel. Accordingly, a two-pronged approach to sampling was employed. An "experienced group" of travellers was obtained by sending an open-

123

ended response form to all 600 members of the American Travel Research Association. This organization is a professional travel body and its members are concerned with tourism research, marketing and advertising. Both because of their occupations and their professional upper middle-class status, these individuals tend to be well travelled. The Travel Research Association has world-wide membership but is dominated by North American professionals. One hundred and ten members of the organization responded to the survey within the specified 2-month period.

A less "experienced" travel group was obtained by asking a small class of 44 Australian arts and social sciences students at Townsville, Queensland to fill in the same survey forms. In addition, each student asked one non-university, non-professional person to fill in the response form. Thus, while the small Australian sample used a limited "snowball" sampling technique and is not in any way representative of the local city or state, it fulfilled the purpose of eliciting responses from a range of people with diverse travel and vacation experiences. In Table 6.1 a brief comparison of the characteristics of the samples is presented. The principal point which warrants emphasis is that while each sample had its own kinds of bias, the composite sample represents a good distribution of age, sex, occupation and country of origin for a

TABLE 6.1   *Demographic profiles of tourist personnel sample, Australian sample and a composite total sample*

Demographic characteristics	Tourist personnel	Australian	Total
Sample size	110	88	198
Males : Females	58 : 42	38 : 62	50 : 50
Mean age (standard deviation)	38·7 (11·8)	27·1 (9·7)	33·6 (12·3)
Geographical locations of persons sampled			
1. Canadian	21%	0%	12%
2. American	54%	0%	31%
3. Central and South America	3%	0%	2%
4. Asian	4%	1%	3%
5. European	3%	1%	2%
6. British	5%	7%	6%
7. Australasian	10%	91%	46%
Occupation			
1. Academic	24%	2%	15%
2. Tourist professional	47%	0%	27%
3. Student	7%	47%	24%
4. Other	22%	51%	33%
Mean no. of countries visited (standard deviation)	18.2 (18·4)	5·6 (7·3)	12·6 (15·8)

sample of its size. The kind of open-ended response requested in the survey was elicited by the following instructions:

> Please provide in the space below [½ page] one positive experience and one negative experience from your own holidays. Please specify the country and place where the experience occurred, the time spent there and your feelings about the experience.

For the Travel Research Association sample all subjects were provided with the following two examples to indicate the kind of response which might be appropriate:

POSITIVE EXPERIENCE

France, Paris, the Eiffel Tower; 4 hours—My feelings: One of the best of my tourist experiences was my first visit to the Eiffel Tower. This had always been a symbol of the international world for me. I felt overawed, like it wasn't really me as I stood there. It seemed much cleaner, less crowded than I had imagined. The other tourists were a nuisance but I felt above them as I sat absorbing the scene for 2 hours. I still think it is a spectacular unique monument. (Young male Canadian tourist)

NEGATIVE EXPERIENCE

Bus tour of Singapore, city centre; 1 day—My feelings: A really revolting experience for me was a crowded, overheated bus tour of Singapore. Graft and corruption were the guiding themes of the tour as we were constantly herded into the shops of friends of the tour company who were all trying to rip us off. Many of the other tourists got on my nerves, thinking nothing of the environment and ignoring the slums in their rush to get a bargain. It was 2 hours of utter frustration for me; a form of capitalism gone mad. (Older female British tourist)

In order to test the reactivity effects of the instructions the Australian sample was not provided with such examples. It is noteworthy that in both samples, many individuals wrote detailed, elegant and enthusiastic replies. Both groups clearly understood what was required in the survey and the effect of the examples for the tourist personnel group chiefly appeared to increase the detail inherent in the replies without noticeably changing their style or content. Not surprisingly the tourist personnel group also used examples from more countries and had been involved in what could be generally termed more extreme (both positive and negative) travel experiences.

While this kind of open-ended data permits classification in a number of quantitative and qualitative ways, the emphasis in this chapter will be to illustrate the tourists' perspective on the topics discussed to date. To gain the best overview of the results any statistical analysis described below will refer to the total or combined sample. There is a necessary caveat which must be observed in performing even simple statistical analysis on this material; namely that the statistics should be treated as descriptive devices summarizing the trends within this group of sampled and should not be interpreted as having any necessary inferential value beyond this sample. Decisions as to the wider ramifications of the material will be left to the individual reader's evaluation of the tourists studied.

The Social Role of the Tourist

The main concern of Chapter 2 of this book was the tourist's role in relation to other traveller roles. From the results of a multi-dimensional scaling analysis of perceived traveller roles it was evident that a sample of quite well-travelled young Australians saw the tourist role as exploitative, insulated, voyeuristic, safe, and conformist particularly in relation to sightseeing, taking photographs and collecting souvenirs. In commenting on their positive travel experiences many tourists from the current study expressed satisfaction when they were not seen as conventional tourists but were treated as interesting individuals or at least representatives of a different noteworthy culture.

A 54-year-old American, a vice-president of a Survey Research Corporation, used as his positive experience a visit to the People's Republic of China:

> The outpouring of curiosity and interest in Americans evidenced by local crowds who turned out in every city to watch any American group was fantastic. The people of China made me feel like a celebrity which I am not.

Another American tourist, a 37-year-old recreation worker, highlighted the same feelings in recording her positive experience:

> In May 1979 I took a four-day tour from Hong Kong to Canton, China. This was a large group tour made up of many different nationalities and age groups. Although I don't usually enjoy highly structured tours that program large groups, this four-day excursion was delightful. I think at this point, the Chinese were not yet saturated with tourists and their tour apparatus was still striving to respond to each and every person in a tremendously personal way. The guides were unfailingly gracious and responsive (even with limited English speaking ability) and anxious to please even the most annoying members of the group. It was a very nice change from the mechanical, if pleasant, response of most group tours.

It also appeared that one or two detailed and satisfying contacts with the local people enabled many tourists to convince themselves that they were reaching beyond the superficial confines of the tourist role. The intimate contact may take the form of sharing food, holding a long conversation or simply co-existing happily in the company of people from another culture. The satisfaction of stepping outside of the tourist role is reflected in all three travel incidents below.

A 30-year-old Canadian management consultant wrote:

> I was taken by my wife's uncle to a local club [Middlesbrough, England]. After only a few introductory remarks, the locals just dove in telling me about England, rugby, football, gambling, etc.—bantering, discussing and involving me, Canada and others. A great way to make a tourist a friend and to make him want to come back again. I felt wanted, an equal, not alone or an oddity.

A Canadian student reported a similar incident involving tourist–host intimacy. She commented:

> One of my best experiences occurred in Antilles, France where we met a young Dutch couple. They were interested in getting to know us because we were Canadians. They were going to Monte Carlo [Monaco] the next day and asked us to go along. We squeezed into a tiny convertible Renault and spent a marvellous day visiting and learning about the country. Between Dutch, French and English we managed to understand one another. It was a fantastic experience to get to know them and they even refused to let us help pay for the gas.

An older North American tourist related a similar positive experience:

> One of my best tourist experience was an afternoon stop at a tea house in a small town in Wales. For something like an hour we were the guests of two old ladies in their living room with a gracious service of hot tea, and home-made cakes and cookies. Our hostesses were so charming it was like visiting old friends.

The negative experiences which many tourists recalled emphasized the dissatisfactions, awkwardness and occasionally guilt which adhere to the tourist role. Many tourists reported incidents in which they were exploited, and even attacked simply because they were tourists. Those who reflected more on the tourist role sometimes expressed a sense of impotence and malaise concerning their presence in the community. A 30-year-old American woman visiting the Virgin Islands commented:

> I felt very threatened by the stark differences between the poor native community and the indulgent tourist community. It made me feel guilty for having a pleasant holiday; bad about their poor conditions; and uncomfortable about "invading" their place.

Similarly a well travelled American marketing manager wrote about the raw shock of poverty in the Philippines:

> My overriding experience in Manila was the sight of thousands of human beings living in cardboard boxes, open fields, trash cans and on the streets within 100 yards of glass studded white walls enclosing some of the most beautiful private and government owned residences in the world. I was distressed and felt totally helpless in face of the thousands of people locked in a seemingly hopeless situation. Had I been willing to give them everything I possessed in life I would have done very little for very few for a very short time.

Comments like these make it hard to support an argument that tourists are necessarily insensitive to the people they see, and the effect the tourist presence is having on the people and the environment. Before further considering tourists' views of the local people and visited environments some attention will be given to tourists' motivation for travelling.

Tourist Motivation

Since the format of the open-ended statements did not directly elicit tourists' reasons for travelling, an indirect assessment procedure was employed to investigate this facet of the responses. Three research assistants examined the critical incidents, both positive and negative, and coded the experiences into five categories. The five categories used were the levels of Maslow's hierarchy of needs. The link between the experiences and the needs was forged by asking the question, "Does this experience principally fulfil a certain need?" For example tourists who placed emphasis on good food and drinking were described as satisfying physiological needs, those whose incidents showed a concern about their self-image were considered to be describing self-esteem needs, while those whose experiences dealt with their personal fulfilment were coded as expressing self-actualization needs. For the negative travel experiences the question asked was altered to "Does this experience represent a blocking or frustration of a certain need?" For example, those whose incidents reflected frustration at not being able to be with people or relate to others were considered to be expressing a concern over love and belongingness needs, while incidents involving threat and assault were coded as safety- and security-related needs. A mean inter-coder reliability score of 0·68 across all the categories indicated close agreement among the coders.

The separate coding of positive and negative experiences affords interesting information. On the one hand it permits an analysis of the positive aspects of travel which can fulfil travellers' motives. In addition the fears and anxieties, as they are exhibited in the frustration of traveller's needs, which detract from the travel experience and which undoubtedly keep many people at home, are also emphasized.

The overall patterns in the total sample were established using a series of cross-tabulation procedures. For the positive experiences it was observed that the incidents reflected the hierarchy of needs as follows:

physiological needs	27%	self-esteem needs	1%
safety needs	4%	self-actualization needs	35%
love and belongingness needs	33%		

A breakdown of the negative experiences, on the other hand, revealed the following pattern:

physiological needs	27%	self-esteem needs	12%
safety needs	43%	self-actualization needs	1%
love and belongingness needs	17%		

This pattern suggests that the motivation for travelling, as revealed by a coding of positive and negative continual incidents, has the properties of an approach–avoidance paradigm. Tourists are attracted to holiday destinations because of the possibility of fulfilling self-actualization, love and belongingness needs and physiological needs in that order of importance. When one considers the avoidance side of the motivational paradigm, a concern with safety is the predominant feature with additional emphasis being placed on failure to satisfy psychological needs, love and belongingness needs, and self-esteem needs. Self-actualization needs, which feature so heavily in the coding of the positive critical incidents, are frustrated in only 1 per cent of the cases in the negative incidents. It can be argued from this that self-actualization needs play a special role in the travel experience. As suggested in Chapter 3 of this book, self-actualization needs reflect personal concerns of the traveller which are largely self-determined. When travellers reflect on their holiday experiences the fulfilment of self-actualization needs is frequently recalled because they reflect largely unplanned spontaneous and personal interests.

The frustration of self-actualization needs rarely features in the negative incidents because, unlike safety and physiological concerns, self-actualization needs are not directly controlled or influenced by other people and the prevailing circumstances. In short, self-actualization incidents constitute a different category or type of tourist experience which is highly valued when it occurs but cannot be directly manipulated by external factors.

Other trends in the data revealed some interesting relationships between the demographic characteristics of the travellers and their motivation categories. In the positive incidents older tourists recalled more incidents involving positive relationships (love and belongingness needs) and self-actualization needs than did younger travellers who gave greater emphasis proportionally to physiological needs. Although the results are slightly confounded because of age, those who travelled more were also likely to emphasize more self-actualization and love and belongingness needs. The less experienced travellers were proportionally more concerned with safety and physiological needs.* Males and females differed only slightly in relation to the positive incidents (male emphasizing relationships and females self-actualization) but the failure of relationships and safety needs concerned the female tourists more in the negative incidents. Occupational differences were not significantly related to the need categories, a finding which supports the view that the tourist role tends to submerge the work identity of travellers (cf. Gorman, 1979).

When the locations of the positive experiences were considered, it was demonstrated that cities were better at satisfying physiological and relationship needs, whereas more self-actualization experiences occurred in non-urban environments. Similarly natural as opposed to man-made environments accounted for more self-actualization experiences while the physiological needs predominated in the man-made settings. For the negative incidents, the predominant settings were man-made or urban environments where there was an overriding concern with the safety and security needs. In fact some 68 per cent of all negative incidents took place in the category safety and security needs/urban setting.

The overall picture which emerges from this comparison of positive and negative critical incidents is one of some complexity. It appears that tourists find satisfaction in a range of settings and motivational categories but the more experienced, older tourists place greater emphasis on the self-actualization experiences. One can suggest some links here between self-actualization experiences and the authenticity approach to tourist environments since it is clear from the foregoing remarks that rural, and natural, settings promote such travel experiences. However, before exploring this relationship it is informative to illustrate the general trends described above with some examples.

Five positive examples, one for each of the need types discussed, provide some insights into the tourists' perspective. A concern with food and accommodation standards constitutes many of the responses of those who were classified as expressing physiological needs. An Australian apprentice who visited New Guinea exemplified such concerns in his comment:

> Five weeks in New Guinea was one of the most enjoyable holidays I ever had, the reason being that it was a different country but the one memorable thing was the food. The food was AMAZING.

---

* A series of partial correlation measures indicated that confounding effects, although present, did not reduce the essential meaning of the relationships discussed above.

A female Australian student typifies those who were concerned with the positive side of safety and security needs, such as holidays involving rest and relaxation. She observed:

> My positive experience was a week on Hayman Island [on Queensland's Great Barrier Reef] with a close friend. Spent a quiet relaxing time together that seemed to last forever. It was impossible to keep track of time—not that we wanted to. It was so perfect, secure and peaceful.

A concern with the positive quality of relationships and a sense of belonging to the visited community are reflected in an incident described by 35-year-old tourist consultant from Canada:

> The highlight of my brief visit to London was the very warm reception I received while at the London Fire Brigade Headquarters. As in any big, crowded city, I had gotten the impression that Londoners were a cold lot. Not hostile to tourists but just caught up in their own struggles and, sort of, unwilling to share their lives even briefly with me. However, the officers at the London Fire Brigade Headquarters freely shared their thoughts of the British economic problems, their feelings towards their jobs and their superiors and their memories of the war years, some of which were obviously not pleasant. They took time out to show me through everything and to answer sincerely my many questions most of which I'm sure they have heard a hundred times. In short, they made me feel in a short time as though we had been friends for years. My whole impression of the English people was thus changed to reflect a more true picture of them.

An account of the fulfilment of self-esteem needs is also illustrated by an incident from England. In this case the tourist was an Australian housewife who had visited twelve overseas countries. She observed:

> My impression of England is that everywhere people seemed to be valued for their own sake rather than from a materialistic, functional point of view. There seemed to be less sex role differentiation than in Australia. My feelings were those of increased self worth and excitement at a new attitude.

The more personal, involving and spontaneous experiences which are featured in the self-fulfilment category can be illustrated by the reactions of an Australian female tourist in Assisi, Italy:

> I walked into the Basilica and was overcome by the simple beauty and inspiring atmosphere of the Church. I had recently seen many of the world's most famous, but none impressed me so much. I am not a

religious person at all but I found myself sitting in a pew thinking of many religious ideals and suddenly found I was praying—more desperately than I thought I ever could or knew how to. And then I started crying. It seemed endless but I experienced relief with some answers in finding myself.

The motives which were revealed in the negative tourist experiences take a slightly different form. In these instances the tourists frequently record feelings of disgust, frustration and annoyance at not being able to achieve their goals or have certain standards of food, accommodation, respect and courtesy.

An Australian student, aged 26, demonstrates the frustration which can arise over matters of food and hygiene. He wrote:

In Milan, Italy, I was annoyed by a fruit vendor who sold decaying fruit to me and many other travellers. Frustrated, I took the matter to the Railway police who said it was beyond their jurisdiction and to go to the "crime police" who in turn said they couldn't help me and to go to some other branch kilometres away.

Some tourists reported considerable difficulty in getting money back for poor food, accommodation, mildewed swimming pools, rotten wine and unsafe rental cars. Occasionally, some tourists saw the humorous side of their experience. A British tourist, himself a manager of a Tourist Board, reported on his car touring holiday of the Republic of Ireland as follows:

I checked into a country guest house and was given a room which smelt damp and musky. I opened the wardrobe in the room and found a pair of false teeth. It made me wonder what might be in my food next morning. I immediately checked out.

As outlined in the general overview of the motivation analysis, safety and security concerns were prominent features of the negative incidents, particularly among female tourists. A British secretary echoes the tone of panic which pervaded several replies in this category. She observed:

During a trip to Jamaica, we stopped at Kingston. The crowds of local street vendors swept like ants towards the tourists, not giving even space in which to walk comfortably. The feelings of being harassed were obvious—the underlying feelings of being preyed upon, gave way to feelings of annoyance. One could literally visualise the vendors becoming violent at our lack of response.

These remarks reflect the concerns about tourist safety expressed by a number of writers on crime in tourist areas (Turner and Ash, 1975; Kent, 1977). While the attacks on the tourists reported in this study were mainly minor thefts, and threatening behaviour, it is clear that tourists may be the innocent victims of terrorism, criminal activity and war (cf. Neville and Clarke, 1979). These threats are understudied but quite significant concerns for many travellers.

Negative incidents which demonstrate alienation and feelings of being an outsider in the midst of others were also reported with some frequency. Two examples from very different places and people illustrate this category. An American professor with considerable travel experience observed:

> Greece was my most negative experience. I spent a week there and found the hotel personnel totally inhospitable, the local folk either frightened or hostile (not sure which) and the food simply not palatable. There was little warmth in relationships. After seeing the touristy sights I was really relieved to leave.

A waitress from Australia visiting an island resort expressed a similar feeling as follows:

> We had saved hard for this holiday and I had dreamed about it for weeks beforehand. We went to South Molle Island for 2 weeks but it was full of honeymooning couples and isolated groups. At meal times my husband and myself sat there wondering what to talk to each other about. I felt out of place with the honeymooners and although the accommodation and meals were first class, it seemed to accentuate my feelings of discontent because I should have been having a good time and wasn't. Good holidays don't depend on tourist facilities but on how one feels inside.

One last comment will serve to illustrate the demeaning events which can befall tourists and threaten their self-esteem. Again it is the rude shock and spontaneity of such events which seems to characterize these kind of incidents. An American woman travelling in Central America simply reported:

> I was walking on the wharf at Manzanillo, Mexico. A sailor who looked to be Cuban spat at me as he approached from the opposite direction.

The feelings of anger and personal insult which accompany such behaviour to tourists need no elaboration. Considerable space has been devoted in the above section to tourists' comments on their travel experiences. It is felt that these comments provide a rich source of data which add complexity and subtlety to the usual pre-planned tightly organized questionnaire approaches to tourist motivation. It should be added that in using the Maslow system of motivational categories, the dominant motive expressed in the incidents has been chosen. There are of course multi-motive incidents reported by many tourists, a finding consistent with the conceptual framework concerning tourist motivation outlined in Chapter 3. While the emphasis in the Maslow scheme is on the psychological satisfaction and needs expressed in the travel incidents it was apparent that some experiences had a strong educational flavour. While it was sometimes appropriate to classify this a self-actualization concern, a better label would be that of obtaining cultural insights. Such incidents bear a close resemblance to MacCannell's 1976 discussion of truth markers, where he argued that some tourists collect information which enables them to perceive and inform others of the "real" nature of the visited environment. Examples which fit this category and which fall largely outside of the scheme employed in this section include the remark of a Canadian executive visiting Europe:

> I spent two days going up the Vars in Western France which gave me an understanding of the people and their habits which until then I had viewed through stereotypes only. I had to endure the Mistral blowing in my ears for close to an hour. I was highly irritated because of the wind continually throwing me off balance and obstructing all other sounds as well as because of the dust it carries. After this experience sitting in a café I understood the reasons for many sights in the area such as why all food and beverage establishments are completely enclosed with glass, why the criminal rate is so high during the Mistral period of the year, etc.

Another clearly educational response is supplied by a 46-year-old American university professor who reports having visited 79 countries. He observed enthusiastically:

> My favourite tourist experience is visiting the Museo Anthropologia in Mexico City, which I consider to be the finest museum of anthropology in the world. Every time I visit I am completely absorbed for hours and find that I easily learn a great amount of information about the diverse cultures of Mexico.

The last two replies also indicate that some of the tourist incidents may be concerned with just one specific environmental setting while others principally involve reports on the social life of the hosts. These two different kinds of topics will be considered in their own right.

The Social Contact between Tourist and Host

Several examples of positive and negative incidents involving tourist–host contact have already been reported. This type of information will not be repeated here, though it should be pointed out that if one quantifies the positive and negative tourist–local contact incidents they occur with approximately equal frequency. The concern in this section, following the discussion in Chapter 4, will be to illustrate the effects of family and friends, fellow-travellers, tourist guides and cultural coping skills in shaping tourist–host contact.

Several tourists reported travel experiences where the increased inter-action between family members dominated the whole trip. On such occa-sions contact with the local people was pushed into the background as the tourists tried to work out the possibilities and problems inherent in their domestic relationships (cf. Crompton, 1979).

A French Canadian researcher writing about a visit to the United Sates re-flects some of these feelings in the following remarks:

> My positive experience was a family trip to New Hampshire. Very in-teresting because it was a much closer communication situation than usual. Such a trip even if it was a short one was the kind I believe should be repeated more frequently.

The self-catering holidays which are popular in many seaside resorts appear to be particularly vulnerable to the criticism that they reinforce and intensify family roles. On occasions these domestic arrangements virtually prevent any appreciation of the local environment, people or holiday.

An Australian housewife and part-time student captures the essence of such situations in the following report:

> We went to Burleigh Heads with plenty of money, rented a nice house and invited my parents-in-law. At this stage we had a daughter 9 months old and I was 3 months pregnant. The in-laws had a good relaxing time while I felt like Cinderella preparing most of the meals, doing all the washing up and in between looked after my baby. The beautiful sunny days went unnoticed. I felt even more irritable when my husband helped because I thought he provided the others with no incentive and allowed them to relax and not me. I felt frustrated and tired and mis-understood by my husband who thought all pregnant women simply neurotic and easily upset.

While the family context provides one social framework in which tourist ex-periences must be viewed, the behaviour and attitudes of other tourists are equally important considerations. Frequent incidents were cited of other tourists' rude behaviour to the locals and inconsiderate responses to their fellow-travellers such as drinking, smoking and vulgar singing. Perhaps the most immediate and striking complaint of all was expressed by a young American female tourist commenting on her fellow-travellers flying from India to London. She reported quite simply:

> I was appalled at their stench.

While one can consider fellow travellers to be supporting actors in many of the travel incidents discussed, undoubtedly the lead roles are frequently

Increasingly, tourists are becoming aware of their role and its exploitative component.

occupied by tourist guides. The guides are in turn vilified and praised, lampooned and treated with respect and generally emerge as critical figures in the minds of the tourists. This emphasis is quite consistent with the importance given to the tourist guides in Chapter 4. Perhaps, though, the gullibility of the tourist in believing the guide was overemphasized in that analysis, since many tourist incidents reflect a kind of tourist sub-cultural awareness in terms of avoiding exploitation, rip-offs and inferior merchandise.

A 60-year-old American magazine editor recalled one such incident in Pompeii:

> The bus tour attempted to push us into a gift shop. The passengers jeered and booed the guide until the bus finally moved on. Any travel executive must be very stupid nowadays to believe that visitors will fall for this.

Some tourists also implicitly rejected the guide because of his role as a kind of cultural pimp, exploiting the locals and profiting from the tourists' money. While it is clear that in many instances a tourist guide exerts a managerial and supportive role in cultural interaction, few tourists would be satisfied with the situation described by one American academic, drawn from his visit to South America:

> In Leticia, Colombia, I went on an Amazon River Tour. This tour consisting of visiting supposed authentic Indian villages was a revolting experience for me. Upon our arrival at each village, the guide would ring a bell to signal the Indians that they should disrobe and put on beads and scanty grass skirts as the tourists were coming. It appeared to me that the way of life, culture, and religion have been destroyed for these Indians. During our study the Indians listlessly attempted to sell their pathetic handicrafts which were what they thought the tourists wanted, rather than be true to their original culture. At the end of the tour, the guide left them beer and cigarettes so that they could wait in a state of stupor for the next group of tourists.

Apart from the tourist guides themselves, tourists noted that many people associated with the travel industry, such as hoteliers, taxi-drivers, restaurant personnel and customs officials, could by their behaviour contribute significantly to the overall impression the tourist gained of the visited people. It appears from the travel incidents that tourists frequently realize that they are making nationality attributions on the basis of contact with a few individuals. This stereotyping process is seen as justifiable, however, because several comments were received which elaborated on the theme—"that is how I saw or found the locals". Many tourists are undoubtedly open to further information and interpretation about their hosts but, as demonstrated in Chapter 4, clear impressions persist and emerge from limited contact experience. This finding should not surprise psychologists as it is paralleled in experimental laboratory situations where very simple distinctions and experiences between groups of people are sufficient to promote labelling and prejudicial behaviour (cf. Tajfel, 1970; Tajfel and Billig, 1974).

Taxi-drivers in particular form one kind of tourist service group whose behaviour was frequently cited as representing the friendliness or interpersonal style of a country. An American woman visiting Mexico city described one such incident:

> On a visit to the hot springs near the airport, I found that my wallet was missing. Close to hysterics, I informed my cab driver and he calmed me and drove me back to my hotel, meter turned off, and waited while I checked my room. To my relief the maid had laid out my wallet on the made-up bed and all my money was there. The cab driver then drove me all the way back to the springs and refused any extra money or fare for the extra ride, saying that he felt it was the least he could do for a tourist in his country. Obviously the hotel maid felt the same way. Ever since then I have remembered Mexico with warmth and gratitude and have visited there often.

Such examples of cross-cultural kindness unfortunately have to be juxtaposed with conscientious attempts by taxi-drivers to exploit and overcharge tourists. Other attempts to please tourists, albeit with a possible cut for the taxi-driver, are however, almost comically inappropriate. An American graduate student visiting Bangkok with his wife hired a taxi with an older Japanese couple after a shared meal. He described the scene:

> After a delightful meal, entertainment, and the company of the Japanese couple, we were again put into taxis for the return trip to the hotel. The taxi driver (who had an excellent command of the English language) proceeded to try to interest me in a massage parlor. Remember, this was in the presence of my wife and new acquaintances. I was embarrassed (as were the other 3 passengers) and repulsed. The driver sensing my uneasiness then indicated that he could also find a parlor for my wife and the other couple!

Salesmen as another group with frequent tourist contact may also markedly influence tourists' images of the local people. And not all salesmen operate from conventional premises, as an American college professor, with the ability to see the humour in the situation reported:

> In Venice, I was in a dark passage along the Grand Canal and found it necessary, candidly, to relieve myself. At that moment I was accosted by 2 young men who grasped my arms, one on each side. Rather than being muggers as I expected, they were intent on selling me some gold

chains, doubtless either stolen, taken or both. Though their purpose was not as alarming as I first thought, it was rather frightening and just a bit embarrassing to be trapped between them, exposed, and faced with the necessity of disposing of them and reassembling myself.

The tourist samples provided relatively few accounts of coping skills in relation to the local people. Many cases of language problems were instanced, but few accounts of non-verbal problems or the impact of different cultural rules were reported. One American tourist described an incident where he was arrested for photographing parts of the city of Addis Ababa in Ethiopia, while an Indian tourist described his difficulty in understanding the Yugoslavian approach to passport visa and health permits. Overall, however, the lack of such reports may reflect the existence of problems at a level which many tourists did not appreciate and such cultural difficulties may lie behind some of the more aggressive, unfriendly responses to tourists described in the motivation section.

While the cross-cultural coping skills described in Chapter 4 were not an important feature of the tourists' positive and negative experiences, the role of guides, service personnel, fellow-travellers and family roles has been amply illustrated. One final point which deserves emphasis in this section is the depth of feeling which contact between tourists and hosts may engender. At times, tourists participate in contacts with the local people which give rise to feelings of gratitude, considerable happiness and in some instances a love of humanity. In the more negative experiences there are often feelings of despair, sadness, inevitability and pessimism concerning human encounters. It will be demonstrated in the next section that the tourist experience in special environments also has the power to generate incidents which are deeply moving.

Tourists and the Environment

There were two prominent features which appeared in the incidents specifically involving tourist environments. First, there was a feeling, as suggested above, of considerable emotional power and awe in special tourist settings. As discussed in the motivation section, experiences which were categorized as involving self-actualization occurred frequently in non-urban natural settings.

A young American office worker offered one of several very positive accounts of the Grand Canyon.

While visiting the Grand Canyon area I was overwhelmed at the magnificence of the Canyon. I now had a real picture in my mind of those many Grand Canyon books I had read as a child. The feeling of "soarability" as I stood on the rim of the canyon at sunrise has never been equalled.

An equally enthusiastic view of a man-made tourist setting is given by a hotel manager from the United States. He described a feeling of anxious anticipation followed by awe in relation to his long-held desire to visit the Taj Mahal.

> I feared my visit to the Taj might be disappointing. It was not to be so. The great outer gates surrounding the grounds remained closed until I had almost reached them. As they slowly swung open the Taj appeared framed in an archway. I have never seen a monument produced by man of such great beauty. No photograph would ever fully capture its elusive grandeur which changed with the changing light and what a delight to discover close-up that it was not all stark white marble, but had intricate decorations of inlaid semi-precious stones in myriad colours. It will always be at the top of my many fond memories of travel.

A second powerful theme in the incidents relating particularly to tourist environments finds the tourists in highly individual and personal contacts with the environment. This personal, and different, experience of the tourist setting is undoubtedly closely connected to the authenticity of the settings as discussed in Chapter 5. It appears that many of the tourists cherish "backstage" experiences of visited locations and frequently these incidents occur at unusual times of the day, in the non-tourist season or in remote locations. The proposal that tourist satisfaction is heightened under conditions of authenticity would appear to be supported by numerous incidents of which the following are representative examples.

An American tourist, the vice-president of a market research company commented:

> In April, 1980 I spent 2 days in Crete. I searched and found a little known chapel in the mountains with superlative fourteenth century frescoes. An old Greek woman got the key from the Mayor of the village and took us up for a private visit. No English was spoken but her pride and our awe were all the communication necessary.

Similarly, an Australian postgraduate student described her first visit to Niagara Falls.

> In early January we crossed the Canadian border and had a wonderful choice of out of season motels at rock-bottom prices. Niagara township looked beautiful in the snowy night and the falls magnificent with coloured lights. Nobody else was about. I'd hate to be there in the tourist season and will savour my own image of the place.

In addition to the themes mentioned above there were concerns about environmental crowding and damage and the overly-organized displays for tourists. One young American office worker commented on a Californian seaside town:

> "Yech!" In a 2 square block area were thousands of tourists all crowding into one "quaint little spot" after another. The shops were semi-interesting but predictably expensive. I felt that Carmel-by-the-Sea was an excellent example of a nice little town that read (and believed) its own reviews.

Overview

The illustrative material presented in the above sections conveys the impression of a host of little incidents which conform to the conceptual considerations outlined in earlier chapters. Of course, such simple incidents are invariably set in a larger framework. Travel is a mosaic of positive and negative incidents fulfilling some motivations, ignoring others and with varying degrees of host contact and environmental appreciation. From the point of view of our social psychological analysis it has been useful to distinguish some of the parameters and variables which characterize these separate incidents and which are critical to the tourist process. As an illustration of the complexity and multiplicity of tourist experience a larger account of one tour group's experience will be presented. In reading this account it is to be hoped that our foregoing social psychological analyses will provide some interesting insight and perspectives, particularly in relation to the social behaviour of the travellers.

The account is provided by an Australian describing an extended overseas holiday.

> I decided to go overseas in 1974 and being rather hesitant about going it alone I decided to travel by ship in the hope of meeting people. I also booked a camping trip which began in London and would take in the Scandinavian countries and Soviet Union, Poland and Czechoslovakia.
>
> The ship was a great idea, everyone under the age of thirty had soon sorted themselves out and into little groups in which we stayed pretty well until the end of the voyage. I was in the group that danced till the band packed up and then after a half hearted attempt to stay up all night would retire and not surface until lunchtime the next day. There was apparently another clique on board who had taken it upon themselves to rid the ship of the deckchairs. Week by week, they disappeared mysteriously at night so that in the end only people over sixty had any claim on the few that remained—the rest of us sunbaked standing up.
>
> The "Russia-Scandi" trip, as it apparently was known to the experienced veteran camping tourers, was a disaster. There were forty three of us, plus a courier and driver—fourteen men in all—the rest, well you

can guess. Things began to go wrong once we left London—we had also left behind the green insurance card. The first few days on the continent were enough for me to realise that I wasn't going to enjoy much of the trip. Most of the group seemed pretty keen to taste all the local liquor they could lay their hands on. We seemed to spend all day driving and all night drinking—often this culminated in the raiding of rival bus groups' tents and the pulling out of any obvious tent pegs as we made our escape.

We were about to leave Berlin when our driver announced that he couldn't find his passport—we searched the bus and then he reported the loss to the police. We spent another day waiting while phone calls were conducted between London and Berlin. Finally, we swapped drivers with a tour on its way out of the Eastern bloc, unfortunately our new driver no longer had a current visa for our next port of call, Czechoslovakia, so it was scrapped! However, he managed to stay sober for far longer than the other driver and so that was a big plus.

Seventeen hours later we arrived in Poland, many of the passengers had whiled away the hours with bottles of Schnapps—and I didn't blame them. We arrived in Warsaw in time to see the sun setting on the frozen camping ground.

By this time a certain hierarchy had been established on the bus. The self elected "leader/stirrer" now allotted various crude nicknames to many of the males. We were also numbered off from one to forty-five. This was in order to allow us to play "Dead ants" successfully. Our "leader" could call out anybody's number at any time and demand a "Dead ant". This meant that he or she was required to lie down on the ground, wave all legs and arms in the air and squeal. This was often performed at railway stations, post offices, museums and other embarrassingly public places.

Another little institution was the Chunder chart—the person who became the sickest after a night of drinking was required to put fifty pence into the kitty—the idea being that some lucky male would be sent to the Red light district in Amsterdam with the proceeds.

Things really began to go wrong in Russia. The front windscreen shattered and we were unable to replace it until we reached Sweden. In Leningrad our group made a lasting impression on everyone. We were in Decembrists Square when our "leader" called out "Group Dead Ant" and most of the group obliged by lying down on the cobble stones of that historic square and waving all limbs in the air, squealed their heads off. The five other tour groups in the Square at the time, all turned their cameras on us!

We attracted even more attention now that we had no windscreen, helped slightly by the sight of our courier who insisted on standing by the driver wearing a bowler hat, barking and howling at passers-by.

Camping life was proving more difficult at the Moscow camping ground—open rivalry was now displayed by the various camping tours that we kept encountering and it was now difficult to keep tents erect all night. Sleep was also difficult as the gathering of hardened drinkers tended to stay up all night and keep us awake with them.

We expected to see our replacement windscreen at Stockholm airport but it didn't arrive. On the way to Oslo the back window shattered, leaving us travelling in a tunnel of very cool air. Most of us bought blankets and huddled in them, crouched below the headrest of the seat in front. The windscreen finally reached us in Oslo but it was too late. The bus refused to go any further. It was when we rang London to get another bus that we learned that our former driver had not lost his passport, he had been trying to sell it in East Berlin. He had also stolen money from many of us, he was gaoled when he reached London. We heard two days later that he had been bailed out by another bus company so that he could drive a group to the ill-famed Munich Beer Fest. He fell asleep at the wheel on the way, the bus overturned, he lost a leg and several of the passengers were injured.

A new bus arrived to take us back to London several days later. We had to drive through most of the remaining scheduled ports of call as we were so behind time. Surprisingly, few objected to this injustice—many of them were booked on the camping trip out and were anxious not to miss it. It seemed that many regarded these trips as the ideal way to "do" Europe. One did the "Five Weeker", that was enough for anyone in the know to realise that you meant the "Russia-Scandi". Then there was the "Nine Weeker" or "Central European", and let us not forget the "Three Weeker", known fondly as "Spain Porchy"—(Spain, Portugal and Morocco). After all that you could fly home secure in the knowledge that there wasn't anything you didn't know, hadn't seen or hadn't drunk anywhere in Europe.

References

CROMPTON, J. (1979) Motivations for pleasure vacation. *Annals of Tourism Research*, **6**, 408–24.

DANN, G. (1978) Tourist satisfaction: a highly complex variable. *Annals of Tourism Research*, **4**, 440–3.

GORMAN, B. (1979) Seven days, five countries. *Urban Life*, **7** (4), 469–91.

HUNT, J. D. (1975) Image as a factor in tourism development. *Journal of Travel Research*, **13** (3), 1–7.

NEVILLE, R. and CLARKE, J. (1979) *The Life and Crimes of Charles Sobhraj*. London: Pan.

PIZAM, A., NEUMANN, Y. and REICHEL, A. (1978) Dimensions of tourist satisfaction with a destination area. *Annals of Tourism Research*, **5**, 314–22.

RUBENSTEIN, C. (1980) Vacations. *Psychology Today*, May, pp. 62–76.

TAJFEL, H. (1970) Experiments in intergroup discrimination. *Scientific American*, **223** (5), 96–102.

TAJFEL, H. and BILLIG, M. (1974) Familiarity and categorization in intergroup behaviour. *Journal of Experimental Social Psychology*, **10**, 159–70.

TURNER, L. and ASH, J. (1975) *The Golden Hordes*. London: Constable.

7

Research Directions

In terms of travel metaphor, the current social psychological approach to tourist behaviour has been something of a novel journey which has avoided some traditional routes, covered some new territory, and revealed many possibilities for further exploration. In particular, by focusing on tourist roles, motivation, social contacts and environmental perceptions, a number of important psychological landmarks in the field of travel research have been overlooked. Notably, the research on travel sickness and jet-lag has not been discussed. A proper account of this phenomenon involves detailed physiological and medical commentary which is outside the scope of the present volume (cf. Reason, 1974). Furthermore, while many studies involving different types of tourists of varied nationalities experiencing a host of tourist environments have been considered, the conceptual approach adopted has not permitted detailed analysis of specific tourist behaviours. For example, little attention has been given to such tourist activities as gambling (Eadington, 1974, 1976), photography (Chalfen, 1979) and shopping (*Time Life International*, 1971).

The omission of such studies has at least one major advantage. By concentrating on the general as opposed to the specific aspects of the tourists' experiences, the present book may be seen as providing an overview of what should be considered in an account of any specific tourist activity. The value of such a heuristic framework may be illustrated as follows. Consider for instance the researcher who wishes to understand tourists' destination choice. The present book would suggest that the following factors warrant attention: the way tourists perceive their role while travelling, their motivation, the preferred amount of contact with the local people and fellow-travellers, and the environmental settings they seek to visit. From these considerations a detailed and comprehensive questionnaire or interview schedule could be derived. The usefulness of using the factors discussed above lies in ensuring a complete picture of the tourist behaviour in question from an experiential perspective.

Interpretation of the data obtained in such a study would not be as difficult as might initially appear because of two critical points. Firstly, it is improbable that the factors specified operate as discrete entities. Although it remains to be established empirically, it is likely that one can obtain a social psychological profile of tourists which links roles, motivation and social and environmental preferences. This offers the possibility of not just a demographic or psychographic profile of visitors (cf. Hawes, 1977; Schewe and Calantone, 1978), but a social psychological profile of tourists. Since such a profile has as its core emphasis the experiences which tourists seek, it can be suggested that such an analysis would have a powerful integrative and interpretive value. One could expect, for instance, to find a social psychological profile which emphasizes the adventure side of the tourist role, the self-fulfilment motivation to travel, maximum tourist–host contact and a preference for non-staged environments. Conversely, there are probable clusters of tourists who are defined by a profile which describes the exploitative nature of the tourist role, the physiological and self-esteem needs, functional tourist–host relationships, high contact with other tourists and an indifference to environmental authenticity.

A second critical factor which makes a social psychological profile potentially useful is its theoretical value. By considering the direction of previous research one not only has a springboard for prediction but a safety net of some value if the research efforts fail. In such circumstances one can set the findings in the context of past studies and attempt to isolate the unique factors which have led to the inconsistencies.

At present there are no completely satisfactory examples of the application of the conceptual approach suggested above. However, an analysis of the social side of tourism in one Australian state, South Australia, has many of the features mentioned (see Steidl, 1977). This report employed a number of multivariate techniques which emphasized the connections between tourist roles (as expressed in tourist activities), tourist motivation (assessed in terms of holiday needs) and what was available in specified tourist regions. While the authenticity issue was not a part of the report and the tourist–host relationships were de-emphasized because it was an intra-Australian study, a social psychological profile of the type suggested earlier emerged. The study identified a cluster of activities such as sightseeing, observing wildlife and participating in active recreational experiences which defined an active, energetic tourist role.

This role was associated with an environmental preference for regions offering diversity and excitement. Such tourists also preferred extensive social contact and favoured the city environments over rural destinations. An attempt was also made to integrate this image with motivational information. An analysis of sensation-seeking using Zuckerman's 1971 scale was undertaken, and a set of items described as a "social and holiday seeking" scale was obtained. A high score on this scale was interpreted as describing travellers who enjoyed new and unusual people and places. From these sources of motivational, social, role-related and environmental preference information, it was possible to identify clusters of tourists from a social psychological perspective. The group identified in Steidl's analysis was one with an active tourist role, who ranked highly on the social and holiday sensation-seeking scale and who preferred urban environments. Other clusters with different social psychological needs and interests were undoubtedly present in the data but were not considered in the report. An expansion of, and refinement to, this kind of work represents the kind of social psychological research which this volume seeks to stimulate. Such work approximates the goal of understanding tourists' behaviour by following an experiential perspective while using the techniques and concepts of social psychological enquiry. It is, of course, also possible to then employ such material, together with economic considerations, for non-academic purposes such as advertising, marketing and evaluation.

Apart from the integrative kinds of studies suggested above, our review of tourist research can be used to direct attention to many under-studied topics. A number of interesting and potentially insightful research areas have received only scant attention, or none at all, in the existing literature. For example, the social status implications of holiday-taking remain largely unexplored.

A number of studies have examined some aspects of this phenomenon (e.g. Nash's study of the social scene in Nice, or Turner and Ash's mention of "place-dropping" in conversation) but a well-rounded account of the interpersonal use of travel remains untouched. Such an analysis could usefully examine the ways in which tourists use their travel plans, travel experiences and travel souvenirs (clothes, mementos and photographs) in their everyday social contacts. It is likely that such data would have to be collected by participant observation, and reported in the micro-sociological writing style exemplified by Goffman. The usefulness of such research would include obtaining information pertinent to the proposals of Cohen and Taylor (1976) who argued that tourists use travel experiences for identity formation and self-development. In a broader context, such work would also be useful in understanding tourist motivation by differentiating tourists who view travel as largely concerned with self-esteem needs and those who do not use their experiences in this way.

As argued in Chapters 4 and 5, there is also considerable scope for further studies of tourist attitude change in relation to the local people and the visited environment. A whole programme of research could be envisaged here. To understand fully the process at work in creating more or less favourable tourist evaluations, it would be necessary to consider tourists of different role types, with different motivational purposes, visiting a range of host communities and environments. In this context considerable use could be made of recent advances in social psychological research concerning stereotyping, group labelling and attribution (Wilder, 1978; Forsyth, 1980; Semin, 1980). While it is unlikely that any one researcher could organize such a programme of studies, it is desirable that research in this field be cumulative. To achieve such an integration of research studies, it is necessary that similar definitions are used and parallel measurement techniques employed to facilitate cross-study comparison. It is to be hoped that researchers can use the studies described in Chapters 4 and 5 as the basis for future work on tourists' attitude change.

One further omission from the research on tourist activities is the lack of any studies in tourists' sexual behaviour. The promise of sexual excitement informs a good deal of tourist advertising and the existence of prostitution in many tourist settings adds emphasis to the need to study the topic (cf. Turner and Ash, 1975). Nevertheless, the impact of sexual liaisons for both tourists and hosts has been largely ignored. Perhaps more studies like that of Cohen (1971) who investigated Arab male–European female relationships would assist in understanding the psychological consequences of such encounters for both parties. A long list of other neglected research topics can be constructed and for those interested in novel areas of enquiry, considerable scope exists in fields such as tourist participation in criminal activities; the design of environments for tourists; training programmes to improve tourists' cross-cultural understanding; coalition formation and group dynamics of travel parties; tourists' health problems; the relationship between life-satisfaction, job-satisfaction and holiday travel, and the role of tourist travel in formal education.

In suggesting such future research directions and topics, it is useful to outline some of the requirements and problems which must be met in this work. It was argued in Chapter 1, following Cohen (1979), that tourist research should be processual (or longitudinal), contextual, comparative and emic. The longitudinal component warrants emphasis in relation to both the work reported in this book and for future studies. The studies examining tourists' attitude changes do not, in general, take a long-range view of the situation. A need exists for future studies to consider the tourists' reactions to the host people and environments not just shortly after the contact experience but 1, 2 or more years later (cf. Smith, 1955, 1957). The contextual emphasis in tourist research places an important framework around our social psychological studies. It serves as a reminder that there may well be significant economic and political frameworks which cannot be addressed by focusing on individual attitudes and perceptions. This, in turn, should generate a healthy respect for the different contributions which can be made by the enquiries of separate disciplines. The comparative approach to tourist research requires researchers to detail fully their methods and the context in which their research was conducted. It is only in this way that sense can be made of findings which are taken from different tourist settings. The final emphasis suggested by Cohen is that of requiring research to be of an emic nature; that is, giving due consideration to the multiple perspectives of the participants. This emic emphasis can be said to have been an important guiding principle in this book, in that a concerted attempt has been made to view tourist behaviour from the perspective of the tourist. Naturally, a more complete picture of tourist behaviour would involve the view of tourist guides, tourist service personnel and the host communities. For those who want to provide a complete account of any tourist and contact situation, an emphasis on the multiple perspectives of all the participants is a highly recommended research goal. Whether or not such groups of people would share the same perspectives of the situation remains to be documented.

There are additional problems for future social psychological tourist research apart from the general considerations offered above. Amongst these issues, the problem of measurement is a critical one. The value of many studies in this area is somewhat insecure due to problems in test reliability and validity. Occasionally standardized psychological tests have been used with tourist samples (e.g. Cort and King, 1979) but such studies are the exception rather than the norm. More frequently, single questionnaires without follow-ups or control groups have been preferred. The meaning of the term replication is at best dubious for most tourist situations, a problem which in turn casts doubt on many of the single-questionnaire studies.

The principal measurement problems which need attention for the development of future work may be summarized as follows. It would be highly desirable to develop a checklist of tourist activities which would be useful in an international context and which contained hierarchical information on preference as well as participation. Such material could then be readily used to assess tourist role identification. These sorts of checklists have been developed by some leisure researchers, but none are specific enough for tourist purposes (cf. Kabanoff, 1980). Considerable attention has already been devoted to the needs of motivation research from a conceptual and methodological point of view. It is only necessary to repeat here that the coding of tourists' experience from a motivational perspective, as illustrated in Chapter 6, represents just one approach to this issue. A similar coding or critical incident technique for anticipated or ideal experiences would be one approach to assessing pre-travel motivation. Alternatively, more conventional forms of questionnaire assessment based on the self-actualization, achievement and attribution approaches could be developed.

Issues of measurement in tourist–host contact situations are also prominent. As argued elsewhere, ratings of interpersonal intimacy and status are difficult (Pearce, 1980; 1981) and the only answer seems to lie in a careful recording of the social encounters from as many perspectives as possible.

Other measurement concerns stem from the chapter on environmental perception, where it was argued that an important dimension differentiating tourists in their attitude to the visited settings was that of desired levels of authenticity. As with a number of other conceptual considerations in this book, it is apparent that at present no satisfactory scale or test is available to assess this proposed variable. It was demonstrated that the variable appears to be theoretically important and can be used to interpret a number of findings, but can only be considered to be properly tested when it has been translated into a number of scales or other operational formats.

While measurement issues are problematic in discussing the path of further exploration of tourist behaviour, they are undoubtedly secondary to a number of important ethical issues. As stated in Chapter 2, tourist research must, to retain credibility, proceed principally in field settings. And yet this implies that one must often approach total strangers and ask for their research co-operation. It is the experience of the writer that many tourists feel such an approach to be particularly invidious. Research questionnaires and interviews are often viewed as a part of the complex, industrial, consumer-oriented world, and tourists do not wish, at least while on holidays, to be associated with such concerns. In future, some camouflage procedures, although not those involving deception, may well have to be used more frequently to counteract hostility resulting from tourists' perceived invasion of their privacy (cf. Webb *et al.*, 1966).

While these difficulties provide a daunting task for future tourist enquiry the rewards of such research promise to be rich. In deciding to study tourist behaviour as a particular facet of human experience one is investigating in microcosm the attitudes, roles and motivations which characterize the more affluent individuals in the modern world (cf. Kavolis, 1970). In this respect a continuing academic focus on tourist experience links one indissolubly to the progress of psychology in relation to these areas of concern. A final recognition of the need to inform tourist research by further psychological inquiry is a fitting note on which to conclude for, as Horace wrote some 2000 years ago: "Coelum, non animum, mutant, qui trans mare currunt".*

* Those who cross the sea change the sky, not their soul.

References

CHALFEN, R. (1979) Photography's role in tourism: some unexplored relationships. *Annals of Tourism Research*, **6**, 435–47.

COHEN, E. (1971) Arab boys and tourist girls in a mixed Jewish–Arab community. *International Journal of Comparative Sociology*, **12**, 217–33.

COHEN, E. (1979) Rethinking the sociology of tourism. *Annals of Tourism Research*, **6**, 18–35.

COHEN, S. and TAYLOR, L. (1976) *Escape Attempts*. Harmondsworth: Penguin.

CORT, D. and KING, M. (1979) Some correlates of culture shock among American tourists in Africa. *International Journal of Intercultural Behaviour*, **3** (2), 211–26.

EADINGTON, W. R. (1974) Some observations on legalised gambling. *Journal of Travel Research*, **12** (3), 1–4.

EADINGTON, W. R. (1976) *Gambling and Society: Interdisciplinary Studies on the Subject of Gambling*. Springfield, Illinois: Charles C. Thomas.

FORSYTH, D. R. (1980) The functions of attributions. *Social Psychology Quarterly*, **43** (2), 184–9.

HAWES, D. K. (1977) Psychographics are meaningful . . . not merely interesting. *Journal of Travel Research*, **15** (4), 1–7.

KABANOFF, B. (1980) Work and nonwork: a review of models, methods, and findings. *Psychological Bulletin*, **88** (1), 60–77.

KAVOLIS, V. (1970) Post-modern man: psychocultural responses to social trends. *Social Problems*, **17** (4), 435–48.

PEARCE, P. L. (1980) Tourists and their hosts: a favourability–satisfaction principle of contact. *Journal of Travel Research*, **19** (1), 13–17.

PEARCE, P. L. (1981) The social and psychological effects of tourist–host contact. In BOCHNER, S. (ed.) *Studies in Cross-Cultural Interaction*. Oxford: Pergamon.

REASON, J. (1974) *Man in Motion*. London: Weidenfeld & Nicolson.

SCHEWE, C. D. and CALANTONE, R. J. (1978) Psychographic segmentation of tourists. *Journal of Travel Research*, **16** (3), 14–20.

SEMIN, G. (1980) A gloss on attribution theory. *British Journal of Social and Clinical Psychology*, **19**, 291–300.

SMITH, H. P. (1955) Do intercultural experiences affect attitudes? *Journal of Abnormal and Social Psychology*, **51**, 469–77.

SMITH. H. P. (1981) The effects of intercultural experience: a follow-up investigation. *Journal of Abnormal and Social Psychology*, **54**, 266–9.

STEIDL, P. (1977) *Behavioural Aspects of Recreation and Holiday Decisions*. Canberra: Department of Tourism and Recreation.

TIME LIFE INTERNATIONAL LTD (1971) *A Study of Customers at Three European Airport Duty-Free Shops*. London: Marketing Research Report, No. 1630, April.

TURNER, L. and ASH, J. (1975) *The Golden Hordes*. London: Constable.

WEBB, E. J., CAMPBELL, D. T., SCHWARTZ, R. D. and SECHREST, L. (1966) *Unobtrusive Measures: Nonreactive Research in the Social Sciences*. Chicago: Rand McNally.

WILDER, D. (1978) Reduction of intergroup discrimination through individuation of the out-group. *Journal of Personality and Social Psychology*, **36**, 1361–74.

ZUCKERMAN, M. (1971) *A Preliminary Manual and Research Report on the Sensation Seeking Scale*. Department of Psychology, University of Delawere, Newark, Delawere.

Index